On Education
for the Authentic

On Education
for the Authentic

Philo T. Pritzkau

Professor of Education
University·of Connecticut

International Textbook Company
An **Intext** Publisher
Scranton, Pennsylvania 18515

ISBN 0 7002 2298 7

Preface

The development of this book is based on the premise that most of the attempts and procedures in instruction and learning are confined to a severely limited encounter with knowledge. An effort is therefore made to suggest some conditions that may liberate individuals from this state of confinement and to provide a confrontation with all phenomena that may extend their sense of existence with meanings.

In the development of this confrontation, efforts are made to indicate how individuals may relate to all the disciplines and areas of knowledge without becoming encapsulated by them. Many conditions are suggested which show the individual as a producer of knowledge as well as being produced by it. It is continually emphasized that the disciplines are not settled structures of knowledge, but rather evolve as the individual relates to them.

In the course of the discussion, many assumptions associated with present practices in the promotion of learning are brought into serious question. Suggested is a continuing inquiry into meanings. Many theories relative to the approach to knowledge are developed. The individual is brought into identity with the disciplines so that he may be involved with them in the development of his being. This suggests that in furthering his sense of existence he must relate himself to what is, and at the same time extract meanings from his surroundings so that he may transform the *what is* as well as himself.

The book relates most comprehensively to the questions about the individual's involvement with curriculum development. Several chapters are devoted to the evolvement of meanings with learners. Approaches to relevant meanings with all learners are described and discussed, the intention being to liberate the learner from a "lineal" concept of approaching meanings so that he may encounter and transform the disciplines and in turn be transformed by them. The conversation with knowledge which the learner develops produces a sense of unity with it as he extends his existence. The material of each chapter is significantly related to the foundations of education as well as the introduction to education. The book can be used effectively in curriculum theory courses as well as in elementary and secondary education and curriculum courses, and in Philosophy of Education courses. This book should also be read by parents and other individuals who are interested in educational development.

In connection with the development of the book's content, grateful acknowledgment is made to Dr. Robert Zais, Assistant Professor of Education, Kent State University, Kent, Ohio, who read many sections of the manuscript and made helpful suggestions. Acknowledged also is the stimulating discussion of graduate students in the writer's classes, which contributed to the development of some of the ideas in the book. The author is especially grateful to Mrs. Eleanor Antan, Consultant in the Curriculum Center, University of Connecticut, for her critical reading of several sections of the manuscript. Perhaps the greatest encouragement and stimulation in the development of much of the content came from Dr. Maureen T. Lapan, Director of Curriculum Center and Associate Professor of Education, Rhode Island College, Providence, Rhode Island.

Philo T. Pritzkau

Storrs, Connecticut
April, 1970

Contents

List of Illustrations

chapter 1

On the Predicament

The authentic may be thought of as that experience in which one has present awareness about himself in relation to his surroundings. The meaning, although difficult to express in words, may be very apparent to the individual as he relates to different experiences. The approach to education for the authentic is not a smooth or settled arrangement. Rather it is beset with all types of difficulties brought about to a considerable extent by the impinging forces of change. More and more people involved in a variety of endeavors are voicing concerns and proposing solutions to the problems of education. All types of proposals are offered for educational direction, and one system after another is put forth as having the ingredients to improve education. The proponents of each advance their claims with the utmost vigor.

It is important that the assumptions underlying proposals be carefully examined for their probable educational effects. But even more important is the need for continued and intensive concern about the quest of human beings for authentic meanings and wisdom. This emphatically suggests that individuals who are most closely involved in education must constantly attend to the liberation of the conditions for learning and inquiry. The teacher is at the center of the tasks which are demanded in the quest for authentic realities. Marshall McLuhan has indicated that all the data on what makes a person more human are not yet in. It is incumbent on the teacher and others involved in education to develop that openness that will invite greater and greater humanness in the approach to learning., Programs, systems, curricula, media, and models should be examined in terms of what they will do to people in their quest for a greater sense of existence.

It should be emphasized that teachers as here conceived are committed to education rather than training or fulfilling the role established by a settled arrangement. In this condition they have become aware of the restraints in established regularities, and have devised ways of liberating themselves and others to illuminate present situations so that they can relate to new meanings and question old ones. They are existential explorers who have encountered new-found vitality and an extended sense of meanings about themselves and the world.

The teacher must become conversant with the external authority and its arrangements. The foregoing discussion of individuals and their encounter with knowledge applies to the teacher and his commitment to education. The external authority is constantly involved in putting people and what they do into ordered arrangements. Teachers are placed in these arrangements. They are trained to find their place here and to train others to do likewise. The design is to involve people in training tasks so completely that there is no time to question where they are or what they are about. Perhaps the first picture that comes to mind as a person thinks about being a teacher is the boxlike container which is the school and its classrooms. Along with this are the various patterned arrangements in the forms of desks, books, workbooks, manuals, courses of study and so on—all of which contribute to the fashioning of the teacher in the ways of conducting "school." Coupled with this are the various controls which establish the hierarchy of communication channels, the segmentation of tasks, the ordered routine, the unquestioned sequential arrangements, and the dividing of people into working compartments. Even with the new mathematics, the practices of team teaching, and the many new programs and "systems," the route of the teacher is clearly defined for him. If he deviates from such a carefully designed system he alone must take the blame. He is involved in a meaningless routine, yet if he makes a mistake in the course of this routine he is censured.

As one views the teacher's role from a position of detachment, it becomes increasingly clear that it confines and funnels his tasks with pupils. Teaching as a condition of inquiry related to knowledge is only vaguely present in the teacher's mind. The design imposed on him consists mainly of taking children through the established training pattern. The characteristics of the role encase the teacher's mind so that his actions become almost automatic. In this condition the architects of the arrangements are not confined to any certain group. Teachers and others become thoroughly and equally involved in fashioning the confining arrangements. They and others have become depreciated to the point where there is almost a complete absence of awareness as to what is happening to them. This ordered condition makes all those occupied with it oblivious to the elements that comprise it. Any moments of reflection about one's being, identity, and extended existence must be entered into quite apart from this established role.

It is quite obvious that teaching for authentic meanings cannot thrive in the conditions just described. The teacher must accordingly try to locate himself in these conditions. How might he visualize himself in relation to the role that has been established for him? Perhaps one of the first things he might do is to ask himself some questions about his location in the role. He might ask, "What am I doing and to what purpose?" "What is happening to me?" Other questions suggest themselves. Who am I and what do I value about myself as I confront with people? What is meant when someone says that you are the teacher? When people say this, do they mean that I can *really* be a teacher, or that I must conform to the plan designed for me? But since they put confidence in me to carry out the design and since I was fulfilling the requirements, was I actually being a teacher? Is the role of teacher merely to fulfill requirements? Perhaps, this is my job and I am here to do it. But is that me—myself? Has my self become a part of the design? Then isn't the design myself? Didn't I prepare for the task of being a teacher, and this is exactly what I am being?

It is, of course, presumptuous to suggest that most teachers would ask themselves questions of this type. In the first place, the tenacious arrangement which has become a feature of the "system" keeps the teacher occupied to the point where thought is eliminated. His time is scheduled with routine tasks so that he is completely encapsulated in the pattern. In the second place, the teacher has become so comfortable with this state of routined security that he fears any interruption to it. The condition of entrapment in the system has prevented any awareness on the teacher's part relative to alternatives. Thirdly, the conditions of individual encapsulation with the system have by design developed a role behavior from which it is difficult to escape— because one is not sure what he is escaping from and where he is escaping to. The condition has in fact alienated the teacher from the self and from the real. The role becomes more important than the person.

The conditions described above are some of the characteristics of the closed system of inquiry. Inquiry is limited by the regularities which become the pattern of some form of institutionalization. The open system, on the other hand, is usually thought of as having the conditions which are largely the antithesis of the pattern of regularities previously indicated. This may be true only to a degree. For example, the captivated ones must discern the conditions of liberation. There has to be a departure from the stereotype of the classroom. The teacher has to be liberated from the confined conditions of institutionalization. The breakthrough, however, is not easy. The open system does not grow out of the closed system. It is not related in terms of an "opposite" condition.

The process of breaking away from the role behavior of the system may overwhelm the individual. Before someone can break away from a condition, he must first know what the condition is. Furthermore, he must be prepared to release his sense of dependence on the old condition before he finds the open system. Perhaps a major clue toward gaining some sense of insight to a condition is to note how the ingredients relate to individuals.

Paradoxically, one might begin to regard carefully a cliché which is mouthed by and associated with the closed system—that "instruction should be based on individual differences." Perhaps the teacher could think again about the original thinking back of this statement and the implications relative to individuals. Then he should consider what the closed system does to individuals—specifically the system in which he finds himself. Proceeding on the premise that individuals are different, he could begin to think about the different ways in which they view themselves and their sense of being. Much of the speculation on the question of breaking through the regularized arrangements of the system is developed in succeeding chapters.

Education for the authentic would suggest that man must seek to relate himself to what is and try to ascertain its ingredients. In this quest relative to *what is* he would encounter anguish as a central fact of life. In this existential conception man is always in question and in the words of Blackham,[1] "always beyond himself, always infinitely more than what he would be if he were reduced to being what he is that in good and evil he is beyond himself always, and this separation is the principle of personal existence." Since man is in question he becomes involved with many questions. The questions engage him as a whole man and are made personal, urgent, and anguished. These questions are more than the traditional questions of the schools but rather involve his separation from himself and his own being and that of the objective world. They go back to the beginning of philosophy with an appeal to all men to awaken from their dogmatic slumbers and discover what it means to be a human being.[2]

In advancing the conception of personal existence it is important that one becomes separated from his own being as well as that of the objective world so that he can produce himself as a particular human being. If this separation did not take place he would be in a state of nothingness, since there is no direction in which he might be extended. He is aligned with the world and his own being in it. In a sense of

[1] H. J. Blackham, *Six Existentialist Thinkers* (London: Routledge, 1952), p. 151.
[2] *Ibid.*, p. 152.

detachment, however, he is not in danger of being engulfed in his own being, and can then view the dense circle from which he has extricated himself and determine therein the area of actual choice and personal experience. He may, therefore, avoid the trap of contriving "illusory objective universal answers." The question is for him alone. There can be no answer that is not his personally responsible decision.

In this state of separation man seeks to understand himself as a particular human being. In relating to *what is* he is careful not to submerge himself with what is because to do so would put him into a settled condition from which no meaning could possibly emerge. If he submerged into a settled condition his mind would receive no illumination relative to *what is* because he has aligned himself with a condition where there is no predicament or conflict and, consequently, he is not in question. How could he be in question when he has become submerged in the settled condition? And what would be the drive toward questions when there is neither a separation from himself nor the condition?

Many of the arrangements associated with education have come to be patterns designed to avoid the predicament or possible anguish that would evolve in an encounter with knowledge. There is a disposition on the part of individuals who are involved in these patterns to depend upon external authority as a means of transcending the predicament. This transcendence has in large part become a principle of operation in many school systems. In effect, it may be a form of the benign altruism that Dewey referred to when he said, "There is a tendency in the present emphasis on altruism to erect the principle of charity, in a sense which implies continual social inequality, and social slavery, or undue dependence of one upon another, into a fundamental moral principle."[3] This principle would provide the route of escape from the freedom of encounter with anguish. At best it is an illusory answer for those who would reconcile their existence with the "regularities" of being. They are then extricated from existing as a question. Dewey adds, "It is well to 'do good' to others, but it is much better to do this by securing for them the freedom which makes it possible for them to get along in a future without such 'altruism' from others."[4] The existentialist perhaps would come out much stronger on this freedom by emphasizing the driving questions toward a breakthrough to "the joke" which the universe has made of man.

[3] John Dewey, *Outlines of a Critical Theory of Ethics* (Ann Arbor: Register Publishing Co., 1891), p. 33.
[4] *Ibid.*, p. 33.

Although the universe has perpetrated the joke on man, the systematization process has tended to hide this condition and has, in effect, put the blame of his dilemma on him. As has been stated man must, therefore, separate himself from himself and the universe so that his mind might become lucid relative to this condition. When this separation has been effected, he may become aware of the location points for a definition and redefinition of himself. He will then be in a position to detect gleams of light in the obscurities which beset him. This will enable him to ascertain some of the operating ingredients of the condition from which he has separated himself.

As man finds himself in question, he becomes involved with the predicament. As indicated before, implicit in this condition is the anguish that develops as a result of man's separation from himself and the universe as he seeks to discover a greater sense of human existence. In the separation he finds himself unexpectedly in a state of despair. In this situation, man shows that he has committed himself—which he and all men must do if they are to escape a meaningless life.

In this state of commitment, man becomes aware of the meaningless life in which he was encapsulated before he separated himself. He becomes aware of the traditional questions associated with the arrangements which engulf him. Figure 1-1 is an attempt to depict the encapsulated condition in which he had his being and to which he must possibly return from time to time in order to more definitively assess himself in that condition. The large circle circumscribes his domain of being. It is very familiar to him as he resembles it. He is not in question because of the familiarity of his surroundings.

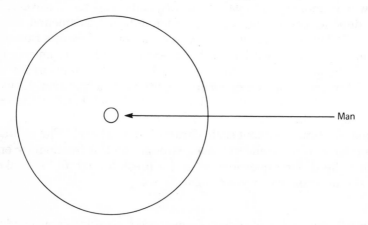

Fig. 1-1. Man in the universe.

He is enveloped in a state of collectivity and to exist he has only to depend on others rather than himself. He really has no responsibility, since everything is in order for him. He has an external authority to guide him. He is a small joke in this universe along with the other jokes. The universe has placed him here, but if anything goes awry the blame is placed on him. He is settled in a situation to which he is unwittingly a contributor. Since he is not in question, and no one else in the condition is in question, everything is well with the world. He is deeply imbedded in this objective world, and he has communication with it. The communication has as its substance a circular sameness, and the interaction remains within the role established for him by the universe. One would think that he is at peace. Yet how could he be at peace when he is in a state of out-of-awareness to the role assigned him? One might then say he is not at peace. Again, where are the sources of vitality that would bring him into awareness to such a condition? He is in effect neutral to any sense of human existence. The universe has provided for him the be-all and end-all of his being. He is reduced to merely being what he is. He is entrapped in a life that is meaningless.

If man begins to reflect on his state of being in the envelopment of the universe, he may encounter a consciousness of his aloneness. He may become engaged with questions about his aloneness. He begins to see himself in his state of being and tries to move beyond himself. The questions are made personal and urgent. He then finds himself in a state of abandonment and separation from himself and his being. Figure 1-2 indicates this state of separation. Obviously the large circle represents the state of circumscription of his being. It represents him as he is. The smaller circles represent man. He has separated himself from himself

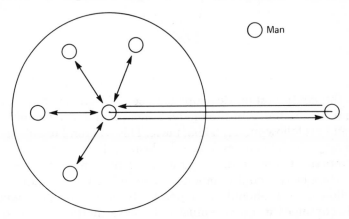

Fig. 1-2. The separation.

and yet retains a continuity with his condition. He retains this continuity so that he may gain some wisdom relative to the conditions that produced him. In the separation he is in anguish because of the infinite responsibilities, without help, that surround him. His anguish becomes aggravated as he sets his aim to define himself into existence as a human being. In these efforts he has to confront himself in the arrangement and yet separate himself so as to extend his personal existence. In the tasks he has set for himself, one fact stands out—that he is responsible for elevating the existence of others. He needs to detect the conditions of entanglement in the arrangement which reduce his fellow-men to be what they are. He is in actuality all men, and his sense of renewal must encompass all men. His definition of himself must be the definition of his fellow-men. They must make one another as they make themselves.

Figure 1-2 suggests the same rigidity as Fig. 1-1 except that in Fig. 1-2 man has begun the separation. In this separation, however, he cannot obliterate the rigid arrangements which exist in the external authority of the universe. As implied before, he has to go back into himself and then out of himself so that he will confront the ingredients that shape him and which in turn he must reshape in order to extend his existence. He involves himself with many questions so that he will be in a constant state of renewal.

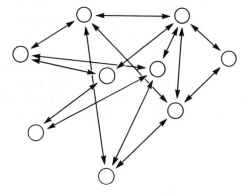

Fig. 1-3. The confrontation.

As the confrontation develops between his existence out of the circle and his existence in the circle, a definition and redefinition of himself and his fellow-men is taking place. This will tend to enlarge the predicament which becomes in fact the heart of human existence. Figure 1-3 represents the predicament as confrontation with it has been effected. Here he is in confrontation with himself as the question as well as his fellow-men. It should be emphasized that the predicament remains. It continues to be accentuated because therein is forged the vitality of human existence. Furthermore, the three figures should not be construed as steps leading to a solution. The confrontation is problem-creating rather than problem-solving, and will multiply and expand the questions relative to the making of a more human human being.

Anguish here is a life-giving tension which not only transforms men but makes them more lucid about themselves. Furthermore, it makes the minds of men attuned to the many messages which flow from an authentic search for being.

Man in his state of separation makes knowledge even as he approaches himself as the question. Knowledge is not "over there," ready-made and waiting to be appropriated. It is encountered even as man encounters himself as the question and pursues it as a source of definition of himself. He makes himself, and at the same time produces the conditions for constant renewal of himself and his fellow-men. In these conditions individuals produce one another by recognizing and moving through the barriers to extended existence. Individuals in effect teach one another as they confront each other in the location places for meaning—which they have ascertained when in a state of separation from themselves and from the settled regularities.

When man begins to study himself he confronts his behavior in many situations—for example, in the regularities of the external authority. Since he has begun to question himself he will attempt to become conversant with his behavior both inside and outside of the regularities. In order to avoid confusion about the term *regularities* some clarification is in order. A term more or less synonymous with *regularities,* is *arrangements.* These terms are used interchangeably along with certain meanings of the terms *systems* and *establishment.* In explaining the meanings here additional terms such as *usual* and *ordinary* are used quite frequently, especially in Chapters 2 and 3. All are employed in connection with man's roles as he functions in an organized society.

Organized society has developed a certain order for those who are part of it. Man makes himself and his knowledge when he becomes aware to what extent his behavior is either controlled or released by the order in which he finds himself. In this connection he begins to ask himself many questions: Do I exist as a unique human being in this condition? Do I identify with the roles in the condition? Do I feel comfortable with the roles? Has this comfort reduced my quest for meaning? Does the role in the organization or regularity suggest an alternative? Has the organization limited my sense of extended existence? Do I have to find the extension of myself outside of the organization or regularity? Have I encountered a sense of anguish? Is the anguish a result of the confinement with the order or the difficulty of penetration of the role for a redefinition of myself? Do I find a point of penetration through the arrangement so that I can begin to develop the *orderings* of my existence?

It becomes clear that as an individual approaches these questions that he begins to find knowledge. It would also seem plausible that he would be in anguish. The meaning of anguish as used here is more than the experience of anxiety. Rather it is a seeking for relevant meanings in the midst of confining conditions produced by the regularities of the external authority. Further, it is a matter of wrestling with the realities of the state of confinement so that the *real* may be found. Realities or "the realistic" as used here refer to the roles arranged for individuals in the regularities of the establishment. The individual who has approached the questions indicated above is seeking beyond the realities. He is trying to locate himself with the "real" and to define himself into a real person. By *real* here is meant the authentic connections toward meaning that are found beyond the arrangements in the establishment. These terms are used throughout the book, and especially in Chapter 3.

Dialogue may be implicit in the encounter with meanings. Dialogue as here conceived is conversation between two or more persons in which each transcends his solitude and accepts his aloneness and that of the other persons, thereby seeking a form of transaction which maintains the maximum freedom of each. In dialogue man freely gives to and freely receives from the person he meets—for no other reason than that each recognizes that he is alone, separate, but able to give and receive from the other.

Kwant suggests that a "real dialogue is possible only if we are willing to be influenced by others."[5] Conversation or dialogue is not simple communication. Furthermore, it should not be equated with the conversational parts of a play. Huebner states that "Communication implies only the transfer of information from one to another, whereas Conversation suggests that the recipient act on this information, reshape it or himself, and continue the dialogue at a new level."[6] Conversation demands are the acceptance and acknowledgment of the reality and value of the other person; not only of his equality, but of his fraternity and solitude. Both, then, "are aware of their duty to discover one another, to help one another onward wherever they encounter one another and to be ready for communication, on the watch but without importunacy."[7]

The order and form of experiences, and the language which symbolizes both, are not simply handed down via an educational process.

[5]Remy C. Kwant, *Encounter*, trans. by Robert C. Adolfs (Pittsburgh, Pa.: Duquesne U. P., 1960), p. 59.

[6]Dwayne Huebner, "New Modes of Man's Relationship to Man" in *New Insights and the Curriculum*, Yearbook Association for Supervision and Curriculum Development (Washington, D.C., 1963), p. 148.

[7]Karl Jaspers, *Man in the Modern Age*, trans. by Eden and Cesar Paul (London: Routledge, 1951), p. 189.

All men have the capability of creating their own form, not simply using that of others. Children use this capability. They are living examples that "to know the world means to sing it in a melody of words."[8] Conversation or dialogue provides opportunity for man to continue to sing of his world "in a melody of words," given the listener who frees the speaker and draws out his experience in new verbal forms. He is free to engage in new insights, and to make them available to the other. Howe emphasizes this point most aptly when he suggests that "The purpose of dialogue ... is to restore the tension between vitality and form, to bring parties of a relationship into communicative relation with one another to shake them free of their conformity and make them available for transformation."[9]

In the approach to dialogue the individual moves out of the "role" behavior which captivates him in connection with routinized and institutionalized tasks. When a teacher communicates in the systematized role he does so in terms of the language of the teacher. When he is in dialogue or conversation he finds himself within the language of himself as a person. In schools, children and youth are often occupied with roles. The talk which proceeds in connection with subject matter is in terms of that content. An individual talks with the teacher in the language demanded by the subject matter.

In dialogue there exists an attitude of "trust of the mind" in seeking meanings. To trust the mind means to give it priority over books, materials, computers, and all manner of arrangements associated with certain forms of school organization. Individuals who promote the conditions in which this priority is present will bring about a new school organization which will liberate them in their quest for greater existence. When the mind is trusted, individuals begin to confront knowledge as a result of dialogue between them.

In true dialogue there exists a condition of "openness to experience." This means that the individual has opened himself to receive messages from others as well as all types of media, with no priority necessarily placed upon one over another. In this condition the school and books may not be considered more important in the extraction of meaning than television, people, and observed phenomena. All must come into the orbit of experience of the individual so that he may exercise responsibility in decisions toward extending his existence.

In dialogue each individual comes to operate as a "first behaver" thus freeing other individuals to be "first behavers." In this condition the teacher, for example, is not placed in a position of demanding

---

[8]Remy Kwant, *op. cit.*, p. 11.
[9]Ruel L. Howe, *The Miracle of Dialogue* (New York: The Seabury Press), p. 64.

behavior from others. Actually he is in a sense a beginner with inquiry into meanings, even as pupils are beginners. This suggests that one should look at and examine his own thinking with meanings rather than isolate himself as the "settled one" with knowledge.

Finally, in dialogue every effort is directed by individuals to liberate each other in the quest for meanings and to approach an integrity with surrounding phenomena. Each one accepts his aloneness and that of the person he meets and freely gives and freely receives in this state. Within this condition the individual trusts and helps elevate the mind of the other. He not only frees himself from the encapsulation of "role" behavior but helps others do so. Through dialogue the first behavers tend to accentuate each other's sense of individual relation to meanings even as they teach one another. In his solitude the individual behaves as the *first one* with meanings, and thus helps others to be first ones with behavior.

Bleak though it may be, there is a glimmer of difference between individuals in their manner of coping with the arrangement of what might be called a closed area of being. This means then that in dialogue there will always be differences among individuals, yet these differences should in effect, bring them *into* dialogue. In the condition of envelopment there are differences, but they are not portrayed in the patterned role demanded in that situation. Rather, the universe with its external authority employs the differences to further reduce the being of the individuals by invoking a state of fear and alienation. In this condition individuals draw away from each other. The only interaction is on a basis of innocuity characterized by a simple sameness in roles.

When one would approach a sense of awareness to the real—the authentic, one needs to consider more than a settled condition or the search for the elements that would place things in order. At the same time he who would seek the authentic would search for a sense of peace. Peace when viewed in this way is not to be equated with a condition of serenity but rather a condition of vitality, renewal, and human elevation. Dialogue as discussed in the above pages should locate elements of the authentic or the real through an intensive conversation in which each one is attempting to follow through toward becoming a more human human being. Conversation and dialogue are used interchangeably here and throughout this discourse.

As each individual tries to relate himself to the state of envelopment from which he becomes separated, he has not only to converse with himself in his present dilemma but also to seek out the many sources of renewal found in the literature which represents the thinking of today and of other times and places. As Howe points out, "one of the first and more simple purposes of communication is to make available to people the knowledge and skill that have accumulated from the study and experience of generations of men."[10] Dialogue must relate not only to contemporary experiences between persons but also to the nature of the accumulated knowledge about the world of persons and things and with the ultimate meaning of them. At the same time, since the content of the world concerns living and thinking, the proposition of life and thought must be brought into responsible confrontation with the requirements of contemporary life. Responsible confrontation of this content through dialogue should bring into focus not only the *what is* for man and his part in it in other times but also the *what is* and his part in it now. This, of course, would relate to both the encapsulation conditions and the liberation ones in which man has variously found himself.

Houghton beautifully develops[11] the focus presented above when he deals with the "Epoch of Atomism" in man's slow and devious efforts to bring about greater humanism. He states, "Humanism has a real meaning to the philosopher. It would seem to refer to those periods in history wherein man has intended to rely on his own resources in his seeking after truth. It has particular reference to that past medieval era in which, feebly at first, cautiously in retrospect, brazenly in fact, certain charismatics ventured to probe beyond revelation while remaining in basic concert with God and sought truth through their own awareness." Houghton[12] traces these efforts of man through Erasmus, Copernicus, Descartes, Newton, and even through Weber and McLuhan. Continuing his discussion on "Atomistic Conditioning" Houghton approaches to the anguished state of man relative to *what was* and, to a large degree, with *what is*, with these observations—"There have been systems and systems, each having charismatic impetus, followed by the inevitable bureaucratization, as ideas, often dynamic and even sensitive, are democratized into inflexible laws to be expanded and enforced."

There is a question about the codification of ideas implied in Houghton's discussion. Could it be that the very charismatic impetus which he seemingly applauds also provides the conditions for encapsulation of humans? It would seem that much more than charisma is called for as men would liberate themselves and open the conditions for continual liberalization toward greater existence. Charisma may be the quality that denies questioning. This would tend to produce the numbness that makes one oblivious to one's existential being.

[10]Howe, *ibid.*, p. 57.

[11]Raymond W. Houghton, "The Focus of Humanism and the Teacher," in *Humanizing Education: The Person in the Process* (Washington, D.C.: Association for Supervision and Curriculum Development), pp. 54–56.

[12]*Ibid.*, p. 56.

The substance of the discussion above makes clear that in a dialogic confrontation with the thinking of men in other times and the present, the distinction between past and present becomes more or less insignificant. As man ventures into a sense of renewal and inquiry and conceives of new conditions of liberation toward greater existence, the external forces of the universe are hard at work in funneling these ventures into a rigid order. The state of separation then has to continue as the anguished condition prevails. Individuals, therefore, have to continue the dialogic encounter so as to bring back the forms of life into relation to the vitality which originally produced them. As Howe[13] points out, dialogue must "restore the tension between vitality and form, to bring parties of a relationship into communicative relation with one another, to shake them free of their conformity and make them available for transformation. Only through dialogue can the miracle of renewal be accomplished in a relationship."

The areas of knowledge are central to the encounter with meanings. Growing out of the living and thinking of men of all times and places are the disciplines of knowledge. Since man is in question he relates himself in his questions to the proposition that the life and thought associated with the disciplines must be approached in his definition of himself. He confronts the content of the disciplines as the generating force and substance by which he builds his greater existence. In the state of anguish in his separation he confronts the disciplines in continuous dialogue. Even as he moves into and out of himself he is at the same time moving in and out of the areas of knowledge which are the product of the living and thinking of men. He penetrates into the *what is* so that he can transform himself toward an authentic existence. At the same time he is transforming the *what is.* As individuals become existentially involved with the disciplines, their minds will tend to become lucid relative to the location places of meaning toward their own renewal as well as the renewal of the disciplines.

A word of caution is in order here relative to one's encounter with the disciplines. If the disciplines are approached as forms of external authority, one may view man in a setting where he may become a creature of purpose in relation to the forms. In this approach the disciplines may be viewed as settled arrangements which encapsulate the individual. This would find him in the situation where his life would become meaningless. He would be trapped in that state of nothingness which is represented in Fig. 1-1.

In the separation of himself from himself and from the objective world, he begins to move beyond and above the disciplines. In ap-

[13]Howe, *op. cit.,* p. 64.

proaching his commitment in the state of separation, he is above the disciplines and yet in continuity with them. In the dialogue which flows with this continuity, he confronts the disciplines and builds them even as he uses them to extend his being. One might say that he locates himself in the areas of knowledge without being enveloped by them.

In his state of separation from himself and the universe, the individual has committed himself toward existence as a more human human being. This means also that he must *evolve* as this particular human being. His responsibility in this commitment and evolvement extends to his fellow-men. Only through a dialogic confrontation with them can he evolve as a more human human being. The sense of greater existence comes about through the extension of existence of all other individuals. In this effort he must become involved with the areas of knowledge. He is thus in relation to the thinking of all other individuals. Throughout the effort a determined attempt is made by the external authority in the universe to codify this thinking into arrangements. If the individual or individuals relax their states of separation, they could easily be enveloped in these arrangements. In this condition they would be depreciated into what may become a meaningless life, becoming less than themselves. Although they would still be physical entities, they would exist only in the state of alignment with the arrangements and would withdraw from the commitment to greater humanness.

The above discussion is analagous to education and the individuals who are involved in it. Most would verbalize that education should be associated with the development of a meaningful life. Most would also agree that education should be central to the evolvement of a more human person. All become involved more or less with the disciplines or areas of knowledge as they pursue their tasks in education. In their zeal in undertaking these tasks, however, they may initially or subsequently become immersed in the regularities of each of the areas of knowledge. The areas arranged by external authority not only encapsulate the individuals with the regularities but also put them into a state of out-of-awareness as to any alternatives. The individual thus aligned with the universe would constantly be reduced to a state of being what he is. At the same time the areas of knowledge would suffer reduction even as he is reduced. Renewal is not in question, since all has been placed in order.

When the individual puts himself into a state of separation from the areas of knowledge, he seeks for the questions which are involved with his development. When he puts himself in question, he approaches the areas of knowledge in this sense of detachment so that he may ascertain the location points of meanings in the areas. Then he can move in and out of the disciplines to assess the ingredients of each that will elevate his existence with further knowledge. His tasks in education thus become the substance and quality for greater existence. For example, he would relate a discipline in science to himself as *being in question with it.* He would inquire as a scientist might inquire so as to extract meaning on the basis of its relation to his extension of himself. In this act of awareness relative to the discipline he would in turn extend the discipline. This is more than appropriating the structure of the discipline as a settled matter. In this condition there occurs a renewal of the individual even as he extends the basic vitality of the content of the discipline. In fact, as the individual inquires into the content the conception of the discipline as a discrete entity becomes questionable. Rather it takes on the ingredients of extended relationships toward human existence. The individual moving outside of himself and thereby becoming more than himself transforms the content of the discipline into a new relationship with himself. In this condition authentic dialogue has been effected.

THE TEACHER AND THE CONFRONTATION

Jourard,[14] in a hard-hitting and illuminating discussion, emphasizes that the most powerful psychedelic agent known to man is not lysergic acid or methadrine. He mentions two that are more powerful. One is to travel to another land and become involved; "the other is the awakened consciousness of another human being." He speaks of teachers as the more powerful psychedelic agents by stating:

> ... I would like to focus upon the self-disclosure of awakened men— teachers. According to this view, a teacher is a man who has been awakened from the illusion that there is only one sane, right, and legal way to experience the world and behave in it. He has become "turned on" such that his imagination is vivid. He can perceive the world as others see it, and more: liberated from convention as he is, he sees what others are blind to. The walls of his capsule have been shattered, and rebuilt so that more world is included in his consciousness.

The teacher must seek to liberate the mind. As suggested before in the closed system, books and materials, organization, and the regularities of the school seem to take priority over the mind. Great teaching will result only if everything which is brought into the conditions for learning is secondary to the mind, and thus to the individual human. The mind as the center of the organism is in a predominant position to relate to and interpret the messages received by the senses.

---

[14]Sidney M. Jourard, "Automation, Stupefaction, and Education," *Humanizing Education: The Person in the Process* (Washington, D.C.: Association for Supervision and Curriculum Development), p. 48.

This priority does, of course, not derogate the importance of books and materials. On the contrary, the priority of the trust of the mind elevates the importance of materials and all types of resource media because they are now viewed as the substance of mind.

Another top priority of the open system related to the trust of the mind is the development of those conditions that invite individuals to a retrieval of meaning from minds. By this is meant the entrance of individuals into a dialogue with one another. Since minds are trusted above everything else, it would follow that to make one's mind an individual needs to relate to other minds. In the closed system this condition is almost absent except as "extra" practices which, after a measure of indulgence, are pulled back into the maintsream of the preconceived regularities of the "establishment." One of the major principles incident to great teaching is always to provide for the conditions that help individuals reach that state of confrontation in which they receive messages from each other's minds. One should hasten to add that the dialogic confrontation between minds will tend to make the mind of each individual. This means that the capacities of minds will be expanded for extended existence.

A top priority of the open system is the provision for a sense of "openness to experience." The individual receives messages from ever so many media other than books and the usual accessible conditions of the classroom. This priority is dominant in breaking through the stereotype of the classroom and school. The school may be one media center among many that furnish messages for the mind. As a selective center the classroom and school should provide conditions that invite children, young people, and teachers to find most of the contact places for meanings beyond its confinements. To illustrate this, one has to make decisions on such questions as to which is more important—the conversation at the sandbox or the "ring around the rosy" game, the observation of the phenomena along the bank of a stream or the reading of the science book.In terms of this priority, the provision for the opportunities of observation of many phenomena and media would be a most pertinent condition in the approach to great teaching and program development in a school. If one makes these provisions only within the limits of the institution, it suggests that he fears "openness" and liberation and thus is developing deprivation places relative to the pursuit of knowledge.

A very important priority in the open system is that each individual should become the "first behaver" in the approach to inquiry rather than look for the other individual to behave first. To be a first behaver is not to be construed as having superior knowledge. In terms of this condition, the teacher is not to be put in a position of having completed his behavior with knowledge only to cause children to be the behavers in learning. Rather the teacher, instead of the children, is actually the beginner in inquiry into meanings. In fact, he behaves with meanings for the purpose of locating the avenues of greater existence. It would follow that the children would also be the beginners or first behavers with meanings. The teacher and the children, as individuals, would all work with the conditions for the extraction of meanings from all the media and phenomena.

With respect to the teacher, this would suggest that one of the criteria of great teaching is *not to teach* in the usual sense. In this criterion the teacher does not become separated from the children, but instead is a behaver with the media and in dialogue with others even as the children are behavers.

In the closed system the principle of the separation of teacher and children prevails. The teacher is the leader and the children, followers. Any deviation from this organization is considered a submerging of the teacher's authority. In the open system, this fear does not prevail because children are not regarded as threats. Instead, they are regarded as possessors of a mind which is central to humanism. In this sense of trust, the teacher's stature is elevated far above that prevailing as a result of the "separation principle" of the closed system. As the teacher's stature is elevated, the children are elevated in stature and dignity. In this sense of elevation no one "gets through" or escapes from knowledge, but each one "turns to knowledge"—to seek further. The condition becomes one that invites individuals to pursue knowledge. Each one behaves in such a way as to open up and expand the avenues toward inquiry and bring into purview all the media to provide a fruitful encounter with the ever-expanding domain of messages. It is hoped that the teacher and other individuals engaged in authentic education will find in the conditions indicated a sense of real identity and a new measure and definition of their existence with knowledge.

The "turned on" teacher constantly seeks renewal through separation from the arrangement. The conditions in which the teacher is encased by external authority have been rather clearly portrayed in much of the preceding discussion. Also described are some of the priorities of a closed system none of which provide for human renewal. As the teacher moves in this condition he may not be aware of what is happening to him. In the situation ordered for him he may become concerned because he is able to fulfill the role without experience and sense fulfillment. Nothing happens to him sensorily or otherwise.

As the teacher stops and reflects from time to time relative to his illusory role together with the tasks associated with it, he may have opened the door ever so slightly on the scene that is. He begins to look at himself in this condition and slips out of it from time to time so that he may experience a few moments of separation from himself. He really is not experimenting but rather trying to discern the ingredients that manufacture his captivity. He sees himself variously as a joke, a slave, and a devotee of illusory goals. He will, of course, try to discern the ways of the perpetrators of jokes, the enslavers, and especially his devotion to the goals. A tinge of anguish, however, could beset him when he gains a sense of illumination relative to a depreciation which is operant on human beings even in their devotion to the goals and goal-setters.

The anguish the teacher experiences in moments of separation is further accentuated when he encounters himself as an avid contributor to his captivity as well as to that of his fellow-men. He thinks of his own comfort in the security of the condition. It has been fun. Also, isn't he getting the most out of life? He has relished being a joke along with the other jokes. Never a care! All is well with the world. But nothing is happening to him. Also, nothing is happening with the substance—the content which he has helped fashion. The content is wrapped in illusory answers even as he is the devotee to the answers. It is depreciated along with the human beings into meaninglessness.

Content as referred to in the discussion is intended to be more than the subject matter of the disciplines of knowledge. Yet it includes subject matter. As the teacher is helping to fashion the content by virtue of his efforts in perpetuating the arrangements that contain it, he is becoming less and less a part of it. He does not identify with it, or pursues it in such a manner that others do not identify with it. All have come to find identity in the security of the regularities of the arrange-ments. An impactful condition for the beginnings of a definition and redefinition of himself is when he senses that his identity with the arrangements produces a sense of occupation with substance which tends to reduce him as a human being. With this sense of awareness the teacher puts himself in a state of separation. Here he finds himself in question and in a state of anguish.

In the condition of anguish the teacher is involved with a commit-ment to an encounter with meanings so that they may become useful to the extension of his authentic existence. Bruner[15] states "The teacher is not only a communicator but a model." In this connection he further points out the importance of inquiry by the teacher by indicating "To be so insecure that he dare not be caught in a mistake does not make a teacher a likely model of daring. If the teacher will not risk a shaky hypothesis, why should the student?" Although the teacher is referred to in the previous discussion as a first behaver with ideas and meanings,

[15]Jerome S. Bruner, *The Process of Education* (Cambridge: Harvard U. P., 1961), p. 90.

the similarity with Bruner's conception is obvious. In the anguish encountered in a state of separation the teacher becomes a first behaver
with meanings by relating himself to the disciplines in such a manner
as to be produced by the content of the disciplines. In turn he goes
beyond the content and will, in effect, redevelop and expand it even
as he extends his sense of authentic existence. As a first behaver with
meanings, he confronts others as first behavers. In this condition there
is a dialogic involvement of individuals toward extending themselves
with knowledge.

In considering the whole question of the anguish that follows
separation, one might become concerned because of the possible isolation which might ensue when an individual has made this commitment.
This state of separation is not withdrawal but rather putting oneself in
relation to the world and knowledge. Being in relation does not mean
that he is confined to an arrangement. It means, that a teacher or individual who puts himself in relation brings himself as a human being to
a confrontation with others. This he can only do in separation; otherwise, he would be in the arrangement and would be aligned with the
others in a state of unawareness to this condition.

One of the most apt illustrations of a teacher in separation is
suggested by McLuhan[16] when he talks about the wisdom of the artist
in the interpretation of any age. "The ability of the artist to sidestep the
bully blow of new technology of any age, and to parry such violence
with full awareness, is age-old. Equally age-old is the inability of the
percussed victims, who cannot sidestep the new violence, to recognize
the need of the artist." If there is anyone who could be said to be in a
state of separation and anguish it is the artist. He does not varnish truth
by associating it with the patterned realism. He is, however, hard at
work relating to the *what is* in any realistic condition; in fact, he is
probably the only one who is aware of it. In this awareness he knows
the future. The teacher who has separated himself from himself and
from the world is in relation with the future. As he relates himself to the
what is relative to the content of the disciplines, he becomes the artist.
He comes to a sense of awareness of himself and others within the
disciplines.

As the teacher as artist is aware of *what is*, he is also aware of the
content of the discipline which is used. In his commitment the teacher
is in relation with the disciplines. In his search for an authentic life he
is in separation from himself in a sense of renewal. Since he has become
aware of the nature of the discipline as used in furthering the arrange-

---

[16]Marshall McLuhan, *Understanding Media: The Extensions of Man* (New York:
New Ameican Library, Inc., 1966), p. 71.

ments, and begins to sense the ingredients that would be associated with a greater human being, he will be in conversation with the content of the disciplines. This conversation will in effect illuminate for the teacher the location places for the extension of his being. He becomes more and more aware of the many messages that come to him from the disciplines and will respond with an elevated vitality, thus establishing a renewed sense of existence with knowledge.

THE CHILD AND YOUTH AND CONFRONTATION

As a teacher assumes a disposition of behaving with knowledge, he thereby invites behavior on the part of the child. The teacher, as he puts himself into separation, becomes open to the many messages which reside in the content of the disciplines. At the same time he is developing an openness to the many messages the child reveals. The child has already had many experiences even as the teacher continues to encounter new experiences. The messages from these experiences will change not only the disciplines but also the teacher.

As a behaver with knowledge, the teacher guards against the child falling into a trap similar to the one from which he extricated himself when he committed himself to a state of separation. He is careful, therefore, that he doesn't arrange for the child the route of liberation which he himself has taken. If he did make such an arrangement, he would in effect be engulfing the child in his pattern of liberation, even if he conceived it as the condition of liberation for himself. This could result in a collectivization of the child. Instead, the teacher puts himself in relation to the child without enfolding him into his sense of being. The child does what has relevance to him.

As the child pursues meanings, he puts them into relationships consistent with his view of things. He produces his own "ordering," cognitive or effective structure or what you will. He is finding out more about himself. He is locating the ways in which meanings influence his search for greater existence. The teacher, in an interpersonal relationship with the child, becomes, in Carl Rogers'[17] words, a facilitator of learning. In this connection Rogers speaks of the irrelevancy of teaching as usually conceived. He says,

> It is most unfortunate that educators and the public think about and focus on *teaching*. It leads them into a host of questions which are either irrelevant or absurd so far as real education is concerned. ... If we focused on the facilitation of *learning*—how, why, and when the

[17]Carl R. Rogers, "The Interpersonal Relationship in the Facilitation of Learning," *Humanizing Education: The Person in the Process* (Washington, D.C.: The Association for Supervision and Curriculum Development, 1967), p. 16.

student learns, and how learning seems and feels from the inside—we might be on a more profitable track.[18]

The teacher and child confront each other in the facilitation of learning. They are not separated from each other as obtains under a condition where one is the "teacher" and the other the "pupil." Each approaches self-actualization through the disciplines even as each confronts with the other in terms of their respective "orderings" of meanings.

The separation of children and youth from themselves is a rather spontaneous condition. Children more frequently than not stand in awe and wonderment relative to the phenomena which they see and hear around them. Curiosity follows and involves them with the phenomena. One illustration of this is prompted by an occasion where several children were intrigued by the efforts of an adult to clean out the leaves from the drain troughs on the eaves of a house. The leaves were saturated with water. As the adult took them out and threw them on the ground, they dropped in muddy clumps. The adult was concerned with the fact that the leaves prevented the rainwater from draining down properly. The children simply asked "What happened?" They were taken by the spontaneous happenings rather than the reasons behind them. They had separated themselves from the facts, sequences and consequences and were absorbed in the totality of the act. Did the experience end here? Not at all. Following their intitial question, they proceeded to bombard the man with all kinds of questions. After a time they even made what appeared to be some rather strange suggestions. In this separation and subsequent inquiry they became more highly involved with the experience than they would have been if they had conceived of it as the way it is. Children viewed the "What happened" in a very meaningful way to them. Important, however, is the willingness of the adult to listen, ponder, and respond. Also, his openness to the children may have had the effect of viewing young minds in a new way. He may have heard many messages which extended his existence with them. Both the children and the adult actually engaged in an act of producing each other. Furthermore, this experience may have helped the adult to separate himself from the regularity so that he could better extend his own sense of viewing people and things.

The school and classroom may envelop children in programs in such a way as to stifle any inquiry relative to their observations of relevant meanings to them outside of the arrangements. What must a child think when the behavior of teachers and other adults precludes all or almost all of the experiences he encounters in the daily eighteen

[18] *Ibid.,* p. 16.

or so hours spent outside of the classroom? What must he think when most of the encounters which are relevant to him are never brought into focus as he pursues his school tasks? More important, what will this type of behavior or lack of it on the part of adults do to him as a human being?

As stated before, children separate themselves from the arrangements of school with comparative ease. They relate themselves to the world so that the world will give them messages far beyond those which have been received by most adults. They not only view the beauty of the foliage in the fall of the year but will relate to this whole phenomenon in such a way that all kinds of thoughts and questions are generated. They wish only that someone will listen to them and respond to them even as they will respond in a real sense of immediacy. Failure on the part of adults to respond to these relevances for a child's being denies him the promises of greater authentic existence. Coupled with this failure is the tragedy of deprivation which is accentuated in the programs of classrooms and schools.

Education must lead in developing the conditions of openness to inquiry and meanings. Educators must separate themselves from the arrangements so that they may receive the messages from the world which will enable education to change itself. Failure to do so threatens the very survival of spontaneity and imagination in human beings. Allen[19] responds to this predicament of youth and schools when he says, "Matched against the incredible prosperity of our society is a mortal threat to its survival. Whether subsequent generations are led toward or away from extinction will depend upon the education we give them or, more exactly, on the education they gain. It is a responsibility that demands that we in education abandon the sanctuary of the grand abstraction universal education has become, the false security of established tradition, and the comfortable certainties of knowledge that lack the humility of wisdom."

Whereas many children may be either distressed or confounded by the failure of the school to be receptive of meanings which seem relevant to them, many youth have become alienated from school. They have separated themselves from school even as they continue to play the role with the arrangements. Since the establishment has continued to be equated with the success image, young people do not feel they can afford to make the total break with it. It is not intended to suggest here that youth would fare better away from the establishment than in it. Some may and others may not. The point to consider is the adamant

[19]Dwight W. Allen, "Youth Education: Promises," *Youth Education.* 1968 Yearbook of the Association for Curriculum Development (Washington, D.C.: National Education Association, 1968), p. 120.

reluctance of the school to acknowledge that it is fraught with conditions which seem meaningless to youth.

When young people drop out of school, they do so usually without putting themselves into question. The school itself also refrains from putting itself into question. As a result both become no wiser than before. The individuals responsible for the furtherance of educational effects do not determine how these effects relate to them. They therefore remain unaware about what education does to them and others. If they are absorbed exclusively with keeping the school as a going concern, they will never really discover the meaning of an encounter with knowledge. By the same token, in this state of unawareness to the potential impact of knowledge on their behavior, they "cop out" relative to the furtherance of education. Reference here is to both the teachers and other school personnel and the youth. Since neither the school and youth have been put into question, one does not learn from the other. Obviously, under these conditions neither the school nor youth will change.

The school should take the initiative in helping youth in their separation to be instrumental in detecting what is and what is not relevant to extended existence in school so that they can help transform the conditions toward extended meanings and realities. Individuals should encourage youth to put themselves into question, even as teachers should put themselves into question, so that each may help produce the other, may expand and give vitality to the areas of knowledge to be encountered.

There is a difference between dropping out of school and consciously separating oneself from the arrangements or institutionalization patterns of the school. As suggested, the dropout who wants "no part of it" does not consciously dwell on the school as having possible relevance for him. The youth, however, who separates himself from himself in the school role may try to detect some breakthroughs in that role. Identity may be found in the school role if the youth can determine which elements of the role may respond to his questions. He may find this identify by being in question and relating himself to the world in such a manner that the world will respond toward his production. The meanings that he has thus realized may be brought into the school role so that the school will change itself. Change here would be greatly facilitated by the efforts of the teachers and other school personnel to make this inquiry by youth possible. An illustration is youth's experiences within and outside a school role. Outside are television, the "hanging around" places, the social confrontations, the quickened pace of the electronic world, the distractions of affluence, and so on. Inside there are subjects, textbooks, outlines, a rather single routine, and regularized arrangements to take people through the route considered school. Somehow there is no resemblance between the inside and outside. Youth seems invited to the outside because of the quickened vitality. He also feels a sense of real existence here. This seems relevant because of its quickened pace, because of its response to more exuberant living.

The teacher and other school personnel need to develop a confrontation with youth, both the dropouts and those who are in but actually separated from existent school realities, to bring into focus the experiences that seem meaningful, using them to revitalize or produce new areas of inquiry. This means that the conditions for relevant educational experiences are not centered in a single area but are found everywhere. The school and youth together can produce and transform the disciplines so that realities may be probed and a real center established for authentic inquiry and existence.

The discourse relative to children and youth and the confrontation has not nearly been exhausted, but enough has been stated so that there should be clarity in the nature of the direction toward education for authentic inquiry and being. The nature of educational inquiry toward greater meanings and relevance for extended existence is developed in great detail throughout the book, but especially in Chapters 2 and 3.

SELECTED READINGS

Berdyaev, Nicholas. *Solitude and Society.* Translated by George Reavy. London: Centenary Press, 1938.

Blackham, H. J. *Six Existentialist Thinkers.* London: Routledge, 1952.

Buber, Martin. *Between Man and Man.* London: Routledge, 1947.

———. *I and Thou.* Trans. by Ronald Gregor Smith. New York: Scribner's, 1937.

Dewey, John. *Outlines of a Critical Theory of Ethics.* Ann Arbor: Register Publishing Co., 1891.

Frazier, Alexander (ed.). *New Insights and the Curriculum.* Yearbook 1963, Association for Supervision and Curriculum Development. Washington, D.C.: National Education Association, 1963. Chapters 1–4, 7–8.

Fromm, Erich. *The Art of Loving.* New York: Harper, 1956.

Gurdjieff, G. *Meetings with Remarkable Men.* New York: Dutton, 1963.

Howe, Reuel L. *The Miracle of Dialogue.* New York: Seabury Press, 1963.

Kwant, Remy C. *Encounter.* Translated by Robert C. Adolfs. Pittsburgh: Duquesne U. P., 1960.

Maslow, Abraham H. *New Knowledge in Human Values.* New York: Harper, 1959, p. 107-119, 151-165, 189-199.

Muessig, Raymond H. (ed.). *Youth Education–Problems/Perspectives/Promises.* Yearbook 1968, Association for Supervision and Curriculum Development. Washington, D.C.: National Education Association, 1968, pp. 26-39 and Chapter 7.

Saint Exupéry, Antoine de. *The Wisdom of the Sands*. Translated by Stuart Gilbert. New York: Harcourt, 1950.

chapter 2

On the Closed System

In order to approach the question on education for the authentic, it is necessary to assess the characteristics of the closed system of inquiry. Some of the basic considerations about this system have been indicated in the preceding chapter. In this section an effort will be made to show how the characteristics of the closed system lead to educational deprivation. By deprivation is meant both the absence of the conditions for educational affluence (those qualities that contain the ingredients for extracting from and with all media the meanings for greater authenticity) and the presence of those conditions that generate poverty in ideas and meanings and narrow the routes to authentic existence. Reference will therefore frequently be made to both deprivation and affluence, since through this conceptualization the ingredients of both should become increasingly apparent in providing the program for educational authenticity.

In the approach to education for authentic existence, the whole question of the institutionalism of the school is involved. Since the school is in fact an institution, the issue of institutionalization has to be faced in relating to the question of learning and inquiry. This is so because the school is the place where much learning and inquiry is supposed to happen. Dewey[1] stresses the role of the institution as exceedingly important in modifying and redirecting the forces which produced it. He states, "Each institution has brought with its development demands, expectations, rules, standards. ... These are not mere embellishments of the forces which produced them, idle decorations of the scene. They are additional forces. ... They open new avenues of endeavor and improve new labors. In short they are civilization, culture, morality." It is clear that Dewey is positive in his approbation of the institution. It would appear difficult as well as undesirable to take exception to the intent attributed to the institution in the above quotation.

---

[1]John Dewey, *Human Nature and Conduct* (New York: The Modern Library, 1957), pp. 79-80.

The quotation, however, suggests a *should* rather than a *what is* or what has come to be a condition. The question here revolves around relevance. The expectations, demands, standards, and so on of the institution may, in fact, have become "mere embellishments" rather than new avenues of endeavor. Perhaps, the perpetuation of systems, many of them outmoded and irrelevant to human existence, has to a considerable and dangerous degree become the central role of the institution.

Mayer[2] questions the force of the institution when he suggests: "We have made the mistake of institutionalizing education and of confirming the teacher. We say we believe in beauty; yet most of our cities are incredibly ugly. We maintain that art is a way of life; yet the poet has no audience. We praise the role of reason, but reason is seldom used in the discussion of social and political issues." The matter of equating education and institutionalization raises the question of the unexamined underlying assumptions of instructional practices which prevail in this condition. These and many other beliefs, proposals, and roles are verbalized by those who are in the institutionalized arrangements without any apparent and conscious regard as to the resultant effects. There appears to be a yawning chasm between what is actually happening to those who are involved. This condition contributes to a closed system and suggests that the practices which prevail operate quite apart from the question of real identity with people. It would seem then that the nature of inquiry called for is that which would deinstitutionalize many of the prevailing practices.

The issues which arise in this connection may relate generally to the following questions:

a. Have the people who are involved in program development for education made any real efforts to ascertain which procedures and content produce deprivation pockets and which produce affluent areas in education?

b. What are the arrangements which have kept them unaware or aware of these effects?

c. What are the possible breakthrough points to develop conditions of awareness to reality as well as to the authentic?

d. In connection with the breakthrough, how and by whom can location places be developed in the media which will provide the conditions whereby individuals may "have things going for them?"

e. What are the roles of staff members and pupils in affecting the conditions of confrontation with meanings and with each other to bring about affluent direction in education?

[2]Frederick Mayer, *The Great Teachers* (New York: Citadel, 1967), pp. 356-357.

f. To what degree is there a determined effort on the part of teachers and other staff members of a school to develop and examine theories of instruction and program development for educational affluence?

These and other questions will need to be approached to enable individuals to locate themselves with all possible conditions as they relate themselves to knowledge. In order to effectively approach this type of inquiry, it is necessary to look at and appraise some of the present conditions for educational direction. It will be necessary, then, to:

1. Appraise the ingredients of the program or curriculum development arrangements of the institutionalized conditions within schools and to attempt to locate one's behavior with them.

2. Develop conditions for the recapture of thought relative to the location places productive of futility. An attempt will be made to assess the ingredients of futility and deprivation both for those who operate daily with these conditions in a knowledgeable manner and for those who operate in it without recognizing them. The conditions here, then, must be of a type of intensity which will make the mind lucid to one's encapsulation with the system and its effect in separating the individual from knowledge. In the conditions or centers to recapture thought efforts would be made also to locate alternatives to the various aspects of confinement associated with "ordered" systems. Assessed also would be the ingredients of release provided in some "ordered" arrangements.

3. Provide for confrontations between individuals and with meanings to ascertain the location places productive of "Things Going For One." Here an attempt would be made to envision breakthrough points in confined arrangements or institutionalism even where one felt he already had things going for him. The point to be made here is that areas of deprivation can be created by individuals and systems that actually have things going for them. An example of this may be questionable grouping practices in school which may tend to segregation relative to opportunities for identity with knowledge. Since rigid arrangements are widely prevalent in schools, it would follow that they are satisfying to many individuals. The confrontation to be developed here should be intense enough to produce a real sense of anguish relative to the conception of satisfaction. The development of arrangements to promote *smoothness* and satisfaction is not necessarily educational. The fact that an individual feels he has things going for him may actually engender educational deprivation. He may, as McLuhan suggests, be "numbed" by the system.

4. Establish centers both in and out of school arrangements for

individuals to identify domains of inquiry or ground of being with knowledge and to ascertain the representative concepts of these domains. Everyone is born into surrounding phenomena through which he defines himself if the conditions are conducive to them. The centers envisioned should enable the individual to relate perceptually to the structure of the phenomena and extend his life space with them and through them to a larger domain of identity with meanings. This condition is also related to the "explosion of knowledge" wherein the individual operating in his domain of meanings will build contact points toward the entrance to knowledge. He should thus find more and more location places for meanings and constantly define himself toward a greater existence with them. This condition is the antithesis of narrowing his domain of meanings as the pupil grows older, which is a pattern often associated with a confined gradational arrangement in schools. The system associated with institutionalism of the school is associated with factors which produce an arrangement of "voids," "traps," and ever so many elements of encrustration and encapsulation of individuals involved with the system. There is a status quo condition which is designed to resist any disturbance or questioning.

The closed system flourishes on a condition of entrenchment. There exists a line-and-staff rigidity in the organization of the system. In connection with this there is a pipeline design for communication. In this design, communication passes down and up. There is a kind of benign verbalism which suggests that everyone is important in the system, but the activated organization belies any authentic indication of it. When there seems to be a need for program development the initiation as well as the need often originates at the top end of the *pipeline.* As the machinery for program development is formulated usually a very sizable part of the staff is included. The involvement of many in the machinery associated with the perpetuation of the system is claimed as a merit of the system. This is a form of efficiency, since everyone has to do his part and the major responsibility does not fall on the "workhorses." Nor is the *top* without support from certain of the rank and file of the staff. The top authority has real support in the vested interests of the staff. By vested interests is meant a feeling of possessiveness of particular subjects by certain staff members. In fact, the system has created the vested interests. In order to maintain itself, the system must have points of concentration to further the design of the institution.

In time most teachers become entrenched with the system because of the security involved. There is real comfort in the numbness associated with the feeling of security. To them, the system carries strength in the fact that it knows what to do and, in effect, has everyone else knowing what to do. After all, there is no floundering and the system moves apace and smoothly.

There are, however, many unexamined practices in the system which may be productive of deprivation areas in education. First of all, the inclusion of most if not all the staff in program development does not guarantee identification with the tasks which have in effect been prescribed. No doubt, these staff members have been members of committees whose objective frequently is to have something on paper at a certain specied time. As a result there develops a detachment from the "grass roots" of content and instruction—the classroom. Program-development tasks thus become removed from the familiar context of identification with children and how they relate to meanings. It frequently follows that program development becomes separated from knowledge as children relate to it. In this condition teachers become separated from an authentic approach to knowledge.

Another condition that may operate toward educational deprivation as a result of the entrenchment of the system is the priority of going *through* the school—six years in elementary, three years in junior high school, and three years in senior high school or some similar arrangement. The system admits children, guides them through the requirements, and then graduates them.

Perhaps the greatest poverty pocket in education may result from the willing acquiescence to the system on the part of many of the staff. The priority placed on a smooth operation of the school has also become the priority of teachers and is exemplified in the classrooms. Teachers then become happily settled in an entrenched arrangement. They find security in going through the paces—the standards, the units—satisfied with forward movement but with very little attention to what the movement does to them as well as to the pupils. Teachers assume that they are making progress and will resist any attempt at raising questions. The system has the built-in arrangements to support them in their devotion to what they consider as smoothness in operation. What has actually been done by the system is to make teachers unaware of the substance which constitutes the program or content prescribed. In fact, the system has unwittingly contrived to put teachers, children, and other people into a state of out-of-awareness to what is real. They have become trapped or collectivized with institutional arrangements. Under these arrangements the means for locating deprivation and affluence in education are largely nonexistent. People have become separated from and are unaware of the elements of greatness in knowledge. They are escaping from knowledge without knowing it.

The closed system places high priority on scheduling. The system operates on the principle of efficiency. Everything seems to be placed in a slot. The major objective seems to provide a neat "ordering" in the program. The priority on scheduling often eliminates any attention to the substance or individuals scheduled. Subjects are used as if they have always been settled arrangements. The priority on scheduling is of such intensity as to eliminate awareness to better and expanded subject-matter content. How do teachers behave in this more or less rigid arrangement? Although a few may express dissatisfaction at the rigidity of the system, most will fall readily into the *slots*. In time—much sooner than they should—they will relish the opportunity of working in an efficient organization. Their tasks are neatly arranged for them and they are happy in the thought that "they know where they are going." They sense satisfaction in the movement ahead even if they are in a state of unawareness as to the effect on people. The resignation to the arrangement becomes so complete that any extended relationships to knowledge which occasionally present themselves are viewed only temporarily if at all, since they are out of the standard subjects in the schedule. If any program development occurs it is usually conceived either from the top, from the department head, or by a body of experts who have been publicized in connection with a more or less fixed system or proposal. No real effort is made to stimulate confrontation toward content development by individuals or groups of teachers in connection with classroom experiences. Curriculum or program development is considered apart from the teaching tasks. The staff as well as the administration resist questioning of going practices. When and if program development is initiated, it is considered as a separate task rather than an opportunity to relate to knowledge in connection with instructional practices. In any event the system of scheduling—the "ordering" of the program for the semester or year—takes priority over anything else.

In the closed system learning is equated with quantification. Pupils are appraised largely on the basis of how much they have done —the number of books they have read, the number of arithmetic problems they have completed, and so on. Not only coverage of material but the quantity of coverage is used as a measure of how much one has learned. Often, too, the teacher is appraised by the principal on the amount of material he has covered. In the system, the teacher, and pupil become so absorbed and occupied with amounts that the idea of recognition of quality receives little if any attention. The system thus again develops the condition of out-of-awareness on the part of staff and pupils in regard to knowledge and its relationships regardless of quantity.

Another form of quantification which is given priority in the closed system of inquiry is the administration of all kinds of standardized tests. It is true that tests give some indication of quality of learning. However, tests are only one measure or form of appraisal and at the most, present only a partial indication of how an individual relates to knowledge and what it does to and for him. Tests may give some indication of a pupil's grasp of material and to what degree he is attaining certain necessary skills. They are, however, limiting in that they do not open up new concepts nor expand the pupil's curiosity with meanings so that he will find new location places for ideas. Tests lead the pupil to be concerned only with quantitative considerations rather than with entering into the marvels of knowledge and its structure. Furthermore, tests somehow fail to make apparent to most pupils that in their relating to meanings they will sense some personal realization. When they find that subject-matter content *has things going for them* they will feel a real invitation to return to it rather than finish it merely to escape from it. Tests somehow generate an attitude of finishing with success, actually culminating in an escape from what is conceived as achievement.

In the closed system of inquiry individuality is associated with the "practical" rather than the theoretical. Since the system of institutionalism places high priority on efficiency, it appraises highly those who possess this quality. The efficient individual is the "one who gets things done." Getting things done becomes allied with greatness in individuality. The person who theorizes becomes suspect. He is viewed not only as a dreamer, but often as a *threat to the system.* This is true even if the theorizer implements the theory into successful practice. Those who have institutionalized the schools have usually been so suspicious of the theorizing individuals as well as theories that there has grown up in educational circles the oft-quoted "It may be all right in theory, but it doesn't work out in practice." This concept has assumed such a commonplace acceptance by many that all theory is regarded by them as impractical. When theories are espoused and examined in educational courses in college, for example, many students accept them as subject matter that is not intended to be believed. Others become indignant with theories and express their feelings with such statements as "I am looking for answers," "I came here to get something out of this course," "I think that is an ideal for which we are not ready," and others.

As was indicated, the individual who theorizes is either viewed as a threat to the system or is ignored by it. The teacher who works with theories in his practices is often viewed as an idealist or a floundering individual who has not planned carefully. The closed system has lost sight of the fact that all practices have originated from theories. It operates on the status quo which has proved rewarding to its perpetuation; it thus has become trapped (and in effect collectivized) with what may actually be *obsolescent* practices.

The closed system of inquiry has become so "entrapped" with the occupation with the familiar as to blind its adherents to mythical and obsolescent factors. One might say that the system has become so aligned with the realistic, the cultural pattern, that it has made obscure the contradictions which operate in that realism. As a matter of fact, the system has produced individuals who are oblivious to the absurdities which they pursue in their occupation with the familiar. For example, an absurdity is practiced and compounded when a teacher refuses to use a poem representing some high-level reflection because grammatical rules are violated by the poet. Another example of an obsolescent and absurd factor is where prerequisites are maintained in certain college courses even if they do not offer meaning to the courses. These prerequisites have to be fulfilled by all students regardless of their previous experiential domain or insights into meanings. Other glaring absurdities and obsolescent practices are the almost universal acceptance of a step-by-step learning sequence for children. The same is true with the continued allegiance to a certain scope in material as necessary for learning. The belief in the practice of having children learn addition and subtraction as preliminary to the approach to number theory is another example of the continuance of a myth. The whole matter of sequence in courses is under question—for example, whether European history should be taken before American history, whether grammar should be studied before composition.

Other myths are somewhat different but are perpetuated by the closed system of inquiry. Among these are the equation of middle class with normal, or the belief that when one works instead of having fun one is making a sacrifice. Another myth and/or obsolescence and absurdity perpetuated by the closed system is that there must be a "required list" of readings to make a literature course effective. As a result some English teachers seem to be constantly at work to determine what shall be the "required reading lists." A myth which has been compounded in practice by the closed system is that conventional materials are more effective than "closed area" materials in promoting high-level communications and idea handling with students.

Entrapment with the familiar occurs as a result of the unquestioning pursuit of "regularized" arrangements of the closed system. Staffs of schools feel a type of security in the familiar paths. Because of the convenience associated with the familiar and the design of the system to keep individuals from "making waves," the matter of the relative degrees of deprivation or affluence generated by the instructional practices will never be known.

The closed system tends to separate the teacher and pupil. In the closed system the roles of teachers and pupils are considered as distinct from one to another. In effect, "the teacher is here and the pupil over there" characterizes this distinction generally. The thinking suggests that the teacher is the giver and the pupil the receiver. One is the teacher and the other is the learner. The teacher is placed in the role of teaching the pupil under the assumption that the pupil learns from "what is handed down." Under this system it is a rarity for the teacher to think of himself in the role of a learner, much less as a learner with the pupils as learners.

In this separation condition the teacher must always know more than the pupil. This is assumed because he is older and more mature and, of course, has gone through the channels of becoming a teacher. The fact that the teacher is supposed to know more than the pupil often introduces some embarrassing situations, especially when a pupil asks questions which the teacher is unable to respond to. To recover from the embarrassment a favorite dodge to the questions is to indicate to the pupils that the "questions are not on the lesson" or "we will take that up later," or some other favorite side-stepping device. The resort is almost always one of face-saving by the teacher. In the system the conditions do not permit the removing of face-saving as a factor in security. After all, isn't the teacher *above* the student?

The separation principle as to teacher and pupil which operates in the closed system tends to create a dualism in responses on the part of the pupil—the one he is supposed to give in the school and the one he gives outside of the school. This condition developes a real area of deprivation for him as well as for the teacher, for neither become wiser relative to the questions they harbor. The dualism prevents an awareness on the part of both teacher and pupil as to individual differences in relating to meanings and what produced the differences. Parenthetically, one might indicate that the closed system is very adept at verbalizing the concept of teaching individuals. The term "teaching for individual differences" is mouthed so much as to become automatized to the point of meaninglessness.

The closed system tends to make the school an induction and "separation" center. The school becomes an induction center from the outside in. There seems to be a precarious disregard for the child's background experiences—the perceptions that are a part of him and which have come from outside of school. The idea of the school as an induction center is characterized by the furor of getting the child ready for school—of adjusting to the school, developing maturity, and so on. The whole matter of "readiness" is verbalized. Readiness in practice becomes more or less a process of preparing children for school irrespective of ideas already entertained by the child.

Another induction term used with older children is *articulation*, a process of making children aware of the role they are to fulfill in the next grade or the next school level such as junior high school. After the junior high school the pupil has to be articulated with the senior high school. Again, this is more or less an induction process. Following this, he is made knowledgeable by his guidance counselor or college personnel about the roles he should perform in college. The whole process in the closed system seems to be that of separation—separating from the out-of-school, separating him from one grade to another, from one school level to another and so on. Most of all, the process separates him from all the forces and media that operate on him outside of the school arrangements.

As one views this process it becomes clearly one of admitting, going acceptably through the hurdles of sequence, requirements, and performance, and finishing to take the next hurdle—all the while going through and in effect escaping from the school and knowledge which the school is supposed to reflect. Always the first priority of the system is to get the child ready for the system and its entrenched "regularities" and then guide him through it so that he can finish. In other words, the system is designed to admit, process, and finish—to help him escape into the world from which he was immunized. After all, this is the "realistic" way albeit lacking in authenticity. Almost absent is the thinking associated with "a turn to knowledge"—for the individual to develop and extend his domain of contact points with meanings—to have these going for him as he relates to deeper meanings. Rarely if at all does a school get itself ready and involved with the child and the domain of experiences he will bring which can furnish, to a large degree, his entrance into knowledge and its ways. Rarely if at all is articulation designed to develop conditions where the upcoming youngsters may indicate their ways of relating to knowledge and help not only to expand the domain of experiences in their background but to generate meanings into the new level in which they are to be involved. Seldom is this group thought of in the light of helping develop educational affluent areas in the school to which they have advanced.

Through the closed system another type of entrenched separation process has come about as between the out-of-school and in-school imagery of the child. One example of this is the manner in which books and materials are supplied and used. As has been indicated before, the child comes to school with a repertoire of experiences. Some of these are quite organized in the conceptual process of the child. Others are relatively unorganized but nonetheless may be important to his further experiences.

When the child appears at the school he is told about its ways and what are some of the roles he must pursue. He is told about the books he will use. In the closed system everything is more or less conceived as a part of it and its perpetuation. Books and materials accordingly, constitute a system. There are the readiness materials, the preprimer series, the primer series, the second primer series, the third primer, the first reader series, and so on. Books of course are necessary, and research has indicated that reading series to some degree will help carry the child into a more or less comfortable attainment of needed skills. The deprivation tactic, however, which develops in the closed system is the manner in which books are employed. First of all, there is little if any reference to books as constituting the experiences and conversation of children and adults who resemble the children in this school and their parents. Furthermore, little effort is made to indicate that the setting in which the children and adults in the book talk about things is the same as the settting in which the children of this school live and talk. These children have "talked" many books in their neighborhoods. If their *talk* had been printed, it would constitute many books. Their experiences in all probability were more varied, and in some ways more interesting, than those of the children whose experiences are recorded in the books in school. Some of these children had no doubt formed their imagery amidst brick and concrete, crowded streets, littered playgrounds and lots. Others had encountered experiences at wooded camps, near streams, with boats, in mountains, wooded pathways, and prairies. The conversation between them would certainly reveal the varied imagery from which perceptions were formed. They would, in fact, be walking books not dissimilar from the books in school. They would not only be perusers of books but recorders of their talk in other books. All the phenomena which surrounds the child inside and out-of-school should form much of the substance of his relating to knowledge. Deinstitutionalized thinking should bring all the imagery of children into play for the further pursuit of meanings both in and out of school.

It should be clear from observations of the workings of the closed system that deprivation pockets are constantly induced relative to education. By the entrenchment of the rigid *program* of regularities of the system the areas for educational affluence are continuously reduced. One such area is in the attitude toward parents and other citizens. The system again develops a line of demarcation between the institution and those it is designed to enlighten. Educational affluence can flourish anywhere if its ingredients are recognized. Then, it must be out-of-school as well as in school. The deinstitutionalization of the school should result in an extension of education affluence areas quite apart from the school center. In fact, to keep parents and other citizens separated from the school limits educational affluence both in and out of the school.

Affluence in education suggests among other effects that through the program of the school and its development one finds relevance for oneself. Since an individual's occupation with various phases of education never is terminated, it would seem logical that every individual can find in it *something going for him.* In the closed system a sizable number of individuals both in school and the community find in education as constituted very little if anything going for them. The system is not designed to stimulate efforts to examine the assumptions under which it operates. This design is accentuated by the practice of separating the school from the community as to its educational effects. Thus it denies this responsibility to the community through its separate character. It is true that various bodies such as PTA's and PTO's and Citizens for Schools have developed. These, however, represent only a semblance of association with opportunities for the development of educational affluence. In the closed system these bodies are a form of verbalization of "school and community cooperation." Mostly they go through the motion of congeniality with the institutionalized arrangements. Very rarely are there any real occasions for educational association in depth with the school. Parent and teacher and people seminars for location of pockets of deprivation and affluence in education are almost nonexistent except where there is a project particularly designed for this and usually supported by an outside agency. The same vacuity exists in people and student relations. Very rarely do people and pupils confront together on educational questions in a seminar setting. In the closed system there exists an out-of-awareness among school people and community people with respect to the type of educational affluence which could result from intensive use of mutual human resourcefulness. The system produces this condition by its nature of isolation.

The closed system tends to separate behavior from learning. The system has developed an attitudinal frame with regard to behavior and learning as existing only when it is *motivated.* The question of how one motivates children to learn is frequently pondered in school circles. The assumption here is that resistance to learning is a built-in attitude of a pupil. It implies also that this *resistance* is behavior and it is not involved with learning but is in fact separate from learning. The system avoids a genuine attempt at explaining what this behavior is. The question above also implies that behavior is motivated—that without motivation it does not exist. Maslow has phrased it quite aptly:[3]

> Contemporary psychology has mostly studied not-having rather than having, striving rather than fulfillment, frustration rather than gratification, seeking for joy rather than having attained joy, trying to get there rather than being there. This is implied by the universal acceptance as an axiom of the a priori definition that all behavior is motivated.

This attitude proceeds on the assumption that the pupil is antilearning conditioned—that he must be approached with fear and trepidation.

Since behavior is viewed in terms of becoming—that is, being motivated and discovered rather than extant now, subtraction and reduction has priority over Being and existence. In connection with this concept, everyone is approached on the basis of deficiency rather than on the basis of a going existence. The whole instructional program is geared to filling the gaps in the deficiency without reference to an existent being who is defining himself.

In the closed system, then, behavior is regarded as a vague and nondescript entity or as one that needs to be controlled. Usually it is not thought of in association with learning. When a pupil does not respond to the program as constituted by the system he is said to be behaving badly. His behavior may be such as produce educational effects in terms of how they seem to him. He may, in effect, be choosing wisely and, if confronted in an honest manner outside of the regularities of the system, he may furnish valuable clues for better program development.

In terms of the system, behavior is usually thought of as having a negative connotation. For example, when one is performing well with subject-matter content he is referred to as "doing well" in his schoolwork. Although educators frequently refer to education as being a change of behavior, they rarely refer to an individual student who is doing well as "behaving more," or "behaving in an inquiring manner," or even "behaving in a valuable manner." The many erroneous conceptions of the question of behavior which are characteristic of the closed system are apparent in such queries as the following:

When do we teach values?
Shouldn't we give time to the inculcation of moral principles?
Isn't there more need for character education?
Why is the period of adolescence such a difficult age?

[3]Abraham H. Maslow, *Toward a Psychology of Being* (Princeton, N.J.: Van Nostrand, 1962), p. 69.

What do you do to keep people occupied when they have finished their work?

When is there time in the day to do all these things?

These and other questions indicate a thinking of behavior as something apart—as something to avoid. Central to these conceptions is that behavior is somehow to be equated with a resistant force. As a result there develops an attitude which associates behavior with the uncontrolled ones, the resistant ones, the peculiar misbehaving ones. Clearly, behavior is not viewed as *extant*-operating here and now without motivation and active in every area of study every minute and hour of the day. This conception is farthest from regarding behavior—active behavior—as the mainspring of a human being and perhaps the truest revelation of either deprivation and affluence areas in education. What a far cry from conceiving of behavior as behaving with one's studies in the locations of meanings! What one should really be concerned about is when and where an individual has stopped his behaving and what influences produced its termination. The institutionalized arrangements of the closed system of inquiry have provided the built-in stoppage places of behavior. These stoppage areas are found in the various practices associated with motivation, measurement, standards, required reading lists, required reading series, and others—in terms of use without relation to human identity—that is, helping pupils behave with and beyond these practices. By stimulating and opening up areas for pupil behavior with the subject, greater dignity would be brought both to the individual and the subject.

Another type of separation which is evident in the closed system is the practice of interpreting and analyzing readings and subject-matter content out of relation to behavior of pupils. Ideas and great thought from various forms of literature are dealt with out of context with particular motivations, feelings, and thoughts of children and young people. Shakespeare's *Macbeth*, for example, is interpreted and analyzed in connection with universal motivations and behaviors which are handled in such a distant manner as to be completely detached from present behavior of pupils. The system somehow contrives rather effectively to separate the meanings of the past and the present. If meanings are brought into the present they are treated in such a way as to be *safe* —that is, not associated with or productive of feelings on the part of the children or young people. There is an absence of confrontation between the thinking of other times and places and the associated meanings which are here and now existent in students. The system has contrived to maintain the serenity of complacency and innocuous pursuit. No wonder many young people treat ideas from great literature as something far away, happening at other times and places rather than occurring here and now as part of all consciousness. In other words, too many teachers continue to deal with ideas and meanings which somehow never find a location place in the present domains of imagery of children and youth.

Getzels and Jackson[4] suggest that divergent behavior is often associated with creativity in youth. Torrance also relates to this concept. In fact, much behavior which deviates from the channels of regularity may contain the ingredients of greatness in thought and action. In the closed system, however, deviational behavior is viewed as anything other than creative. Most often, as has before been indicated, deviational behavior is regarded as forms of violation. Getzels and Jackson cite research which shows that teachers generally prefer convergent over divergent behavior even if the students who exhibit divergent behavior are highly intelligent. The separation design which operates in the closed system here is that deviational behavior is generally regarded as out of step with prevailing instructional practices. One might say with a reasonable degree of authority that this type of separation is instrumental in furthering educational deprivation.

The closed system tends to develop an exclusive prescription which associates school meaning with the "realistic" rather than the "real" or authentic. Programs of learning are designed to be congruent with the apparent state of reality. The logic operative here is to gear the pupil to relate to *what is* as the goal and to take him to a sense of completion with the *what is.* There is little if any disturbance stimulation toward a questioning of the *what is* and to contemplate what should be. The program of learning proceeds only by the guidelines of charted areas. Uncharted areas relative to reality are treated as *out of bounds* and not approached as successful practices in schooling. Some degree of contemplation is encouraged, but it is held in the bounds of a patterned arrangement.

The key term which is associated with the regularized arrangement is "to be realistic." Individuals are exhorted to be realistic in their schoolwork as in other tasks. This is the exhortation to students and it is also applied to teachers. If a teacher begins to ask questions about the regularized practices, someone might say to him, "Yes, but we have to be realistic." The one who says this rarely stops to examine the components of this statement. In fact, the statement implies a "stoppage" condition in thinking. It is a deprivation statement by virtue of its closure implications. The whole situation of what comprises the verbal-

[4]Jacob W. Getzels and Philip W. Jackson, *Creativity and Intelligence* (New York: 1962).

ized "realistic" may find its dimensions in the familiar, even the absurd.

The unexamined concepts of "the realistic" may produce elements of disaffection. These conditions are resident in an elusive and subtle manner in obvious school practices. They may be associated with the concepts about "coverage of subject matter," "the unit method," "course completion," "finishing school," "learning one thing at a time," and others. These are the stock-in-trade of the closed system—the institutionalized managements. When people begin to discern the elements of disaffection in their operating environment, they may have acquired the initial disposition to inquire further relative to the realism which has produced these elements. Perhaps, through this inquiry they may begin to visualize the pockets of deprivation to which they have unwittingly contributed and to discern some routes to educational affluence.

In the closed system the exclusive prescription or design for learning seems to relate to a form of perfect fulfillment. It is a dream which haunts man's days like a timeless mirage. The closed system of regularities regards fulfillment as a form of idealized condition—a form of ultimate realization—which is unattainable and which is viewed in that light. It is the antithesis of *Being*—of behaving now in a condition of self-actualization. The closed system views the self in a state of out-of-awareness of the condition of actuality. This concept places man in a condition of the Dream of Eden—that man is unthreatened. This would place him in a state in which there is no pain, no weariness, and no disappointment. As viewed in this condition, there is no conflict between what man wants to do and what he ought to do. It is a numbing condition in which the mind becomes too relaxed to relate to the obvious. It says in effect, "What will be, will be, and one might as well make the best of it." One might as well "get the most out of life."

The system prevents the mind from becoming lucid and transparent to truth. In a previous section it was suggested that the closed system separated the out-of-school phenomena which influence the imagery of individuals from the experiences which are carried on inside of the school. The system has thus been instrumental in creating deprivation pockets in the guidelights to understanding. The effect has been to produce a rigidity in the mind which obscures the guidelights to insight relative to such aspects in human experience as tensions, anxiety, conflicts, fear, and guilt.

The guidelights to understanding have been clamoring for man's attention and concern. Literature, philosophy, painting and music have been engaged in an all-out protest against the optimistic notion that all is well with man. Artists have been articulating this new and sobering wisdom for the last hundred years and more. Men should be eternally grateful that they live and work in this period when artists, philosophers, and poets, refusing to varnish reality with the gloss of wishful thinking, have spared nothing in their depiction of the human situation. Other guidelights would be exemplified by the insights drawn from one's encounter with other men's thought as emphasized by Buber through his I-Thou and I-It concepts. Kierkegaard has tried to point to a sense of man's uniqueness before God. Man can, therefore, attempt to define himself existentially in this uniqueness in an I-Thou relationship with God. Buber would add the necessity of man's sense of community with the world in his encounter with God. Buber carries the conviction that man's earthly task is to realize his created uniqueness through I-Thou relationships.

Encounters such as those emphasized by Buber should become a reality as teachers work with teachers, as children confront other children, as youths relate to other youths, and as children and youth enter into dialogue with teachers. Furthermore, these encounters should become a continuing pattern of confrontation as between these individuals and groups and the thinking of the poets, philosophers, artists, and others. The minds of the teachers and the children and youth should become transparent to the truth; that a clear and lucid discernment of what they are, where they are, and what they must become should pour through them as sunlight pours through clear glass. For many their minds, however, give them no such service. They find neither the world nor their own lives intelligible. To put it another way, the closed system has subtracted their minds even from this finding. To be sure, at times they feel some great unknown thing is demanded of them, but they either do not know what it is, or they think there may be a way to this demand which is vaguely represented in the regularized or institutionalized arrangements. They find themselves fighting something but do not know what it is. Thus their emotional life is more or less awry. They and others are anxious about rather then at peace. The closed system provides specific conditions—those of regularity and of settledness. Since these individuals are already anxious, the regularized arrangements can lead to acute anxiety because they intensify the conditions which are with them all the time. Their minds become what might be called a shambles, and produce opacity instead of lucidity because no alternatives are in the offing. The only recourse to them is a "flailing away" at unknown objects since the conditions are all within deprivation. The individuals are children of the culture as patterned by the "separation points," the "realistic," the "regularities," the "obsolescences," and the obscurities of the closed institutionalized arrangements.

As individuals find themselves in the predicament where their minds do not give them the service that they need, inescapability becomes their life pattern. They resign themselves to inescapability without becoming aware of the ingredients which comprise this condition. The condition, through the cultural and educational deprivation caused by the closed system, arises from the ensuing precariousness of their lives in their physical, moral, and spiritual dimensions.

Physically the lives of those patterned by the closed system are confronted by *fate and death.* "Fate" stands for everything about life that affects it decisively but is unpredictable, irrational, and beyond control. Fate is constantly driving individuals ineluctably forward from less to more, from past to future with each moment vanishing even as it is appearing. Psychologists have indicated that men begin to die even before leaving the womb. Thus there is in this precariousness of life a perpetual perishing, a relentless nullifying of existence, a continual subtracting from individuals the life that is given them, a reduction of men as they expand, and a lowering of one's stature as it rises. Subtraction and reduction in the process of a fulfillment have priority over existential *being* in the closed system of inquiry. The priorities have produced a form of deprivation which accentuates perishing over being, depreciation of existence over individual extension in definition, a subtracting of life rather than a giving and receiving of it, a reduction rather than an extension of individual uniqueness, and a further deterioration of statures as they are formed.

In the moral dimensions of the precariousness induced by the closed system, men see only that they are threatened by the fact that they do not live as they feel they should. As a result of this condition they begin to take on proportions of guilt. They feel guilty about the opportunities they have let slip by. They are guilty and concerned about self-precautions they feel they should have taken. Thus they are beset by many conflicts, anxieties, and unknown factors as to produce a form of devastation through which they lack any clues for direction toward self-identification. All these elements may impinge on individuals with such magnitude as to cause them to seek recourse to meaning anywhere except through themselves. They then continuously escape, come back, and escape again. Their efforts to resolve their existence is a relentless exiting from it. It appears to be an admission that they are not adequate to the task of approaching understanding of the predicament into which they find themselves as a result of living according to designated regularities.

To reiterate the effect of the closed system, one should indicate again that it operates to make obscure the ingredients of depreciation of the individual. Confining the mind to the regularities of the system has the effect of constantly narrowing the route to meaning. By failure to provide alternatives which make one receptive of the message from literature, philosophy, and the arts for the mind to become lucid to absurdities, obsolescences, and the many pockets of deprivation, the system reduces the avenues of possibilities through which human experience must be understood. The dimensions of self-affirmation are negated by the arrangements. Meaningless restraint seems to pervade all behavior. There is a steady depletion of energies in the pursuit of tasks which rest on unexamined assumptions as to their validity. Finally, the system restricts the accessibility of the cultural content to the point where it fails to excite, to convince, and to inspire.

SELECTED READINGS

Buber, Martin. *I and Thou.* Trans. by Ronald Gregor Smith. New York: Scribner's, 1937.

Goodman, Paul. *Growing Up Absurd.* New York: Random House, 1961.

Klopf, Gordon J., and William A. Hohman (eds.). *Perspectives on Learning.* New York: Mental Health Materials Center, Inc., pp. 73-106.

Marcel, Gabriel. *The Existential Background of Human Dignity.* Cambridge, Mass.: Harvard U. P., 1963.·Chapters 7 and 9.

Skinner, B. F. *Walden Two.* New York: Macmillan, 1962.

Vale, Eugene. *The Thirteenth Apostle.* New York: Scribner's, 1959.

Weber, Max. *The Protestant Ethic and the Spirit of Capitalism.* New York: Scribner's, 1958.

chapter 3

In Quest of Extended Realities

Reality as usually conceived might be considered a measure of one's existence. Existence, as defined in this context, would be that state of realization where one identifies the direction which the culture holds for him. This need not be construed as a state of conformity but rather as a condition where one may recognize both the constricting and liberating elements and thereby detect the routes by which he may break through the cultural barriers to extended meanings. This is not to be construed as a contradiction. Whenever anyone identifies his possible direction in the culture, he has to a certain extent become knowledgeable about it and has perhaps recognized some of its limitations. Accordingly, in detecting the limitations of the culture, he is cognizant of its ingredients and is in a position to detect certain avenues of separation from it. Or, rather, the separation becomes a return which has released somewhat novel connections.

When one becomes knowledgeable relative to what the culture requires of him, he will be in the position to ponder some of the possibilities for him as an individual. He recognizes what he must do to be "in step" with the requirements. Furthermore, what is more important is that this knowledge also clarifies to him under what conditions he might be "out of step." It would be obvious that if he were not knowledgeable about the requirements of the culture, he would not know which of his behaviors would be "in step" and which "out of step."

That one has detected the limitations should constitute a new ground of development. It would seem to be logical that if limitations were apparent to the individual, he would contrive new ways to either remove the limitations or proceed to a ground in which new directions could be developed.

By ground here is meant that state of self-actualization of one's being which develops and extends his domain of location places for greater existence with the media and substance of knowledge. The domain is there and becomes extended as he continues to reach integrity with the phenomena surrounding his existence.

SEEKING REALITIES IN THE "USUAL" AND "REGULAR"

In the thinking about extended directions in or through the culture, it is important to view the behavior of individuals or groups as they are being "realistic" with the ordinary or the usual routine of existence. As individuals encounter one another, they usually do so in terms of the roles to which they have become accustomed. The roles are associated with the concept embodied in the expression, "The way things are." As individuals converse about their regular sense of occupation, there is no question about what their behavior should be. It has become habitual. The behavior together with the role is anticipated by the individuals even before they engage in conversation.

At times individuals in their conversation joke about themselves. There may follow a period of viewing themselves as "at odds" with respect to real existence. This is a form of "breaking away" and occurs with a sense of caprice. Perhaps they felt the need for a little excitement. Thus they engage in a session of breaking out of the usual, the ordinary. This may occur in periods of light socializing or entertainment. There may even be a satisfaction in laughing at themselves. They may detect some absurdities in the roles they pursue. When the "show" is over, however, or when the levity is terminated, each one comes back to "the way things are"—to the ordinary. Each one again disperses to the usual. The individual's realities continue to be the regular arrangements. He never seriously intended them to be anything else.

It would, of course, be ridiculous to assume that the "breaking out" of the role as indicated above should be a permanent form of behavior. The condition, however, illustrates the usual association with reality. The "breaking out" is simply an escape for a period with no intention of seeking realities outside of the ordinary and regularized patterns of behavior. Although absurdities are sensed in passing, their impact remains obscure. No one became wiser relative to his lot in the "role" designated by the way things are.

Assuming that the "breaking out" of the role would be with more basic issues, would the impact be more penetrating than in the capricious view indicated? Many examples seem to suggest a negative answer. One of these is where practices and thinking are being questioned but only in the committee room or classroom. Often the questioning is not intended as such, but merely a form of mental exercise which might be excused in a condition isolated from the arrangement. Another example is where individuals spend an evening discussing somewhat innovative ideas and then return to their usual roles of routine thought as they leave. Soon the innovative aspects of their discussion are forgotten.

As one views the approach to realities as suggested in these conceptions, it becomes more and more apparent that there is no real effort to inquire into the nature of the realities. Furthermore, the attitude of complete comfort in shrugging off absurdities indicates a rather rigid condition of encrustation which confuses the possibilities for existence with the real or useful. In fact, the "trapped" condition takes one into such a state of unawareness that resources other than those associated with the "regular ones" will have to be found or developed to produce that sense of detachment which will reveal some directions to a breakthrough. The big question that enters here is "How can a breakthrough be contrived through a condition when one is not aware of being in that condition?" Furthermore, how will new resources be located when the individuals are fully occupied with those which are congruent with the existent realities? The approach to these questions and others at first appears discouraging. Perhaps some form of sacrifice or risk-taking is needed. Perhaps there are some great individuals who are not content to bask acquiescently in the familiar arrangements and will probe beyond the existent realities.

DEVELOPING CONCEPTS ABOUT EXTENDED REALITIES

If one were to proceed inductively to bring about some different concepts about extended realities, he could continue to "go in circles," since the sense of detachment that might be needed would be suppressed in the route of the implied logic. The whole area of logic usually operates with *what is* rather than on uncharted speculation. There is, no intent here to deprecate the subject matter and wisdom associated with logic. What is intended is to encourage greater search for the "real" rather than to reside in a state of patterned contemplation.

When someone exhorts us to "be realistic," it is not only important but imperative that the implied reality be examined for its content. Shouldn't the exhortations to realism as conceived be regarded with a degree of apprehension, especially if they imply a "stoppage" condition in thinking?" It is hardly admirable that thinking on the part of those who are acceptant of this exhortation frequently seems to reach a state of resigned completion. The major clue toward gaining insight to true reality is perhaps the openness of the recipients relative to the type of exhortation indicated. By openness is meant that the hearers of the "let's be realistic" statement do not accept it as a completely valid dimension of realism. The hearers by this openness invite an extension of thinking about the so-called realistic to effect a state of confrontation with its exponents. The questioning involved in the confrontation would tend to examine assumptions in the thinking about realism. The hearers then become responsible in helping the exponent of realism examine his conceptions of it. Furthermore, the state of *confrontation* will tend to reconstruct the hearers' conception of realities. Thus the expositor of the initial reality and the recipients engage in a condition of producing one another toward a higher experience of being than would have been possible had there been a resigned acceptance of the so-called realism.

The question associated with the nature of approach to meanings about reality is vitally related to the extension of knowledge as between teacher and student. At the same time the development of concepts of reality is integrally tied up with programs for learning and the extension of one's existence. It is obvious that all too often programs for learning are designed to be congruent with the apparent state of reality. This reality is frequently associated with a tenacious approach to "achievement." "Coverage" here takes priority over intellectual reflection. The mind becomes submerged and is replaced with *things*. Readiness is used as a system which is, in effect, a state of out-of-awareness to children's thinking and relating to meanings. Courses and subject matter are so organized as to allow no time for thought.

It would seem that the extension of reality should equate with the authentic. This may be dangerous, however, because it may suggest an ultimate condition. Authenticity could imply a form of preconceived "objective" which might establish limitations to extended meanings. Also, it is difficult to define. What is authentic to one individual may not be so to another. For example, material well-being may be considered most authentic to some individuals, whereas others may regard it as a condition that closes off the routes to greater existence. Authentic reality assumes different meanings in terms of perceptions of individuals. Again it becomes clear that the authentic may be arrived at by individuals within the enculturation process. In other words, to be authentic to some is to do the "right thing." Others, going to another extreme, conceive of the authentic as "being different." In the one case, those who are acceptant of existent reality see no desire or no avenue to escape from *what is*. Those who conceive of the authentic as "being different" may find themselves escaping from reality without being cognizant of what they are escaping from. Characteristic of this form of escape from reality is the practice of changing patterns of a program or instruction for the purpose of being different or "up-to-date." Another form of escape is a decision by individuals or groups to promote change in a school situation by making accessible more materials and equipment without considering behavior in the situation.

A number of advocates of change seem to be convinced that a change in the organization will do it. Both of these conditions lack an overriding ingredient—that of mind. These individuals regard elements other than the mind as the most important. Absent is a condition in which the trust of the mind is involved. No condition is apparent which would emanate from the individual's concept of self—how he locates himself in the new arrangement. No condition seems apparent that would define the individual as a "first behaver" in the pursuit of knowledge. Certainly there appears to be no disposition to suggest that the making of a mind may occur through the confrontation with other minds. Could it be that the enculturation process has been as effective in keeping both those who stay within and those who escape from reality in a state of *out-of-awareness* of the "real"—the authentic?

SOME CONCEPTS ABOUT THE AUTHENTIC MAN

In approaching a discussion on concepts about the authentic man, it is important not to set up a *type* or an ultimate condition. Rather the discussion here is related to a distinction between what is usually considered as realistic and what is thought of as real. There is quite a difference, for example, between the expressions "he is a realistic individual" and "he is real." The former refers more or less to one who has the situation in hand and who is pursuing a course which is for the time and place regarded as a regular one. One the other hand, when a person is referred to as being real, he is viewed more or less as standing out beyond the ordinary. Although he may possess many of the characteristics of the "realistic" individual, he has shown qualities that give him a certain uniqueness. In other words, he possesses a type of singular identity which, although derided by some, seems to stretch and stand up beyond the derision. The real person is what Maslow[1] refers to as a growth-motivated person. The individual referred to as the "realistic individual" is a "finishing" person. He has come to rest with the surrounding conditions. All the time he is more or less occupied with beginning and finishing. After he has finished, the completion is usually final with regard to a particular task. No new relationships are established relative to it. In fact, tasks are chosen in which the beginning and end are envisioned. When new tasks are chosen, they are in the same

[1] Abraham H. Maslow, *Toward a Psychology of Being* (Princeton, N.J.: Van Nostrand, 1962), p. 28.

category as those completed. His reality is contained in the beginning, following through, and completion of tasks. Another factor which characterizes the realistic person is that the mode of operation of the tasks he chooses is established. It is not intended that any questions arise relative to the tasks. Obviously no questions are raised by him as to relationships and extended meanings regarding these tasks. He is usually not a growth-motivated person.

The person who is conceived of as real, may be cognizant of all the elements of tasks as envisioned by the realistic person. In addition, he goes beyond the tasks in seeking fulfillment. Fulfillment resides only partially in the finishing or completing of tasks. He looks for further areas of existence with the tasks and develops conditions which will produce a compulsion for him and others to move into the type of inquiry which will open doors to greater meanings. Maslow indicates that "this person rather than coming to rest becomes more active."[2] Maslow emphasizes further that to the real person,

> growth is, *in itself*, a rewarding and exciting process, e.g., the fulfilling of yearnings and ambitions ... ; the acquisition of admired skills, like playing the violin or being a good carpenter; the steady increase of understanding about people or about the universe, or about oneself; the development of creativeness in whatever field, or, most important, simply the ambition to be a good human being.

It would seem that a possible approach to the authentic is the evolvement of a more human human being. The growth objective of the authentic man would be to seek out the incredients which constitute images of humanitarian greatness.

As one would approach a greater sense of the authentic, it would appear that although he can live rather effectively with the cultural milieu, he would not be acquiescent to this state of being. He would appraise the patterns of the culture in terms of its "closed" and "open" conditions. In areas where "stoppage places" or deprivation pockets to existence are clearly evident, he would attempt to help people discover the avenues for a breakthrough. In the previous discourse, frequent reference is made to possible breakthroughs in the settled arrangements of the culture. Perhaps readers begin to suspect that to extend one's existence one must always be in an unsettled state. It is not our intention to create this impression. An unsettled condition per se may reach nowhere. The one who seeks for authentic existence is indeed settled, but the conditions of settledness are such as produce comfort with tensional inquiry. This point is emphasized by Allport when he says:

[2]*Ibid.*, p. 28.

"Growth motives . . . maintain tension in the interest of distant and often unattainable goals. As such they distinguish human from animal becoming, and adult from infant becoming."

In ascertaining the ingredients of a greater sense of humanness, it is imperative that the person who seeks the authentic penetrate the residuals which reduce human dignity. He becomes rather settled on this objective. He will promote penetrating concern and inquiry about the "collective thinking" which categorizes people as totalities rather than individuals.

When seeking to ascertain the content which contributes to greatness in images of a more human human being, a person must necessarily become involved with subjects, whether men or material. The one who would seek the authentic will move away from these subjects so as to ascertain the ingredients of their composition. If he does not move away from them, he may become so involved and enmeshed with the arrangements that he may not recognize the "threads" and "tentacles" that keep him there. He will need to question most intensively the "ordered" or sequential arrangements to which he may have been subject. He then may need to establish his sequence of inquiry, especially if he senses that prearranged sequences are in effect keeping him from examining alternatives that may provide the messages and media by which he might approach a greater existence.

The individual who would approach greater insight about the ingredients of authenticity, accepts the human association with mistakes. If he is afraid of mistakes he doesn't invent—because invention is fraught with mistakes. Furthermore, mistakes as usually conceived may be an appraisal which emanates from the arrangers of the ordering of content in the closed system. In this condition the devotion of individuals to correcting "mistakes" becomes so tenacious that messages of great magnitude fail of reception by default.

In the closed system the route of inquiry is so clearly ordered that it is difficult for the individual to fail to see a mistake he has made. An implied priority in the system is that it is "mistake proof." The messages to which he should be receptive are clear signals which are built into the system. Any deviation from this constitues an infraction and the individual who is guilty is viewed as frail and, in a sense, pitiful.

To the individual who would approach the authentic, the system may be the mistake. In order to extend his existence, he would, then, have to become a sort of chronic mistake-maker. He has to be at rest with this tensional condition. In this condition he is becoming responsible because he is trying to locate the ingredients of the mistake—the system and what it does to humans. He cannot exit because if he did he would obscure the routes of wisdom both for himself and others relative to the conditions residing in the system. Perhaps he detaches himself sufficiently to locate the ingredients which tend to perpetuate some areas of deprivation for those who are in the closed arrangement. In this detachment he may reflect on some questions regarding the depreciation and elevation of human beings. The questions would no doubt relate to differences in individuals, the trust and mistrust of the mind, and other factors. In approaching responsibility with the questions he could perhaps develop some occasions for dialogue with other individuals. As a lonely one he could approach other individuals in their sense of solitude and loneliness. He would encounter the "closed" with an ever-increasing openness. He would need to do this as a "first behaver" in his inquiry relative to himself.

What may seem to be elements of lucidness relative to his mind may be discerned by others as having obscure ingredients. Other individuals as first behavers may then propose alternatives for him, thus opening up areas of inquiry which he may well pursue. This very condition may have a reverse effect in that it could actually provide lucid discernment of extended directions by those who proposed the alternatives.

It may become clear to an individual that perhaps in his deviance he may have become closed to most important alternatives. When a person conceives of himself as being the open one or the authentic one, he may thereby be defending a closed condition. Perhaps the one who is recognizing his comfort with a closed condition may be the real opener to inquiry.

In confrontation situations with others, the individuals who would approach an understanding of the authentic would appraise the roles of people in the culture in terms of the extension of human existence. This suggests that the stabilized roles of the culture are examined and appraised largely on the basis of their relation to humanitarianism. Roles which seem to operate on the grounds of political feasibility or on expediency alone would, of course, come under serious question as to their relevance.

The authentic one would keep himself lucid relative to stereotyped conceptions of images entertained by himself and others. The conditions which associate images with class, hierarchy of values, position, power, prestige, and other extrinsic factors would be laid bare as to their limiting effects on the authentic. An incident which illustrates an allegiance to images was described by a staff member who was asked to find an outstanding candidate for a vacancy existing in a particular college. As a candidate was brought in for an interview, most staff members were rather satisfied with the qualifications displayed by the candidate. Some members, however, were not satisfied, and gave as one of their reasons that the candidate did not have the image of that position. On being questioned further as to their meanings, they referred to his manner of dress, his appearance, and other rather superficial details. No reference was made to other qualifications such as his research, his knowledge about people, his manner of relating to inquiry into knowledge, and others. They were not aware as to the authentic. As one becomes more lucid relative to his behavior, he thereby is becoming a more healthy individual. As he studies the more healthy individuals, he should in all probability arrive at more valid concepts regarding the authentic as he confronts with others. The one who seeks the authentic has the responsibility to help those who exhibit a disposition for extending the dimensions of being to probe further for a clear identity with this condition.

If one would approach the authentic he would put himself in a position of confrontation—a dialogic and interprobing condition—with many of his fellow-men. Occasional use is made of the term "confrontation" in one context or another. The context in which the term is most prominently indicated here is the act of producing oneself. The one who would seek for the authentic would put himself into a condition of confronting with others as well as with the values he entertains. He accepts complete responsibility relative to his own behavior which has become his concern. In this effort, however, he will attempt to develop the conditions whereby he becomes cognizant of the disposition of those with whom he confronts. As Kierkegaard has stated with emphatic impact, the individual who would approach himself as a man becomes conscious of himself with all the attributes of being this particular individual and assumes it as part of his responsibility. At this moment of choice of himself, he is in complete isolation and yet in complete continuity, for he chooses himself as product. In this sense of detachment he is producing himself.

As the individual confronts others, he is not only detaching himself from the patterns and questions that seem to influence him but is also helping the confrontees to do likewise. He is cognizant of and comfortable in the "creaturely bound" relationship with others. He puts himself in a state of community without collectivity in the confrontation with others. He accepts this same condition on the part of those with whom he confronts. Each individual then is that "Single One" which Buber has most aptly discussed. The confrontation here is on an *I* and *Thou* dialogic relationship. The I or Thou is *You* as the "Single One." What are you doing which will help you be *You*? What are you doing to help along those coinditions that will enable children to think intensively and reflectively about the phenomena through which they need to define themselves? Have we examined the possible tenacity associated with a priority for "coverage" so as to effect a release toward thought? Have we provided avenues whereby children and young people become sensitive to the messages from all media? Are there provisions for observations which will bring into purview all subject matter so that individual children and young people will derive key questions through which they may extend their existence? Have we, then, contemplated the degree of separation in thinking as to their key questions and ours to the point of helping them as individuals (Single Ones) to produce not only themselves but also you and me?

The real conditions of confrontation exact from each individual those strengths which make for a boldness of viewing and entering into the ultimate problems of life. Associated with this is the requisite of the dimension of seriousness and profundity of living (or, perhaps, a capturing of the "tragic sense of life") as Maslow so aptly states. The indidivual needs to establish for himself the conditions in which he begins to develop relationships which will locate, for example, the *stopping places*—the barriers—to the extension of his knowledge in terms of how the world seems to him.

The above condition will be an invitation for the seeker of the authentic to probe beyond the perimeters of regularity. Perimeters then vanish. Now he needs to think beyond the subject, its marks, and its prearrangement which are usual requisites of going through the curriculum of the institution. Within the process he will find many possibilities for the acquisition of knowledge. He will take care, however, that the assumption associated with acquisition of knowledge does not become absorbed in the priorities associated with completion of courses and credits. He will see that the ends to be served do not become associated more with a measurement of the student's progress in the curricular continuum than with the confrontation of knowledge itself. In the confrontation for production of himself and others he must be constantly alert to the ingredients of this regularity so that he will not be trapped into a condition of out-of-awareness relative to it.

As one proceeds toward greater authenticity he increasingly develops an openness to experience. The entire discussion in the previous sections relative to one's approach toward the authentic might suggest the extension of the location places in one's ground of being. This extension depends on the openness to experiences by teachers and others which would, in turn, tend to develop openness to experiences on the part of children and adults.

Figures 3-1 and 3-2 are designed to indicate the differences in approach to knowledge as between those who have settled attitudes about experience and those who entertain an openness to experience.

As will be noticed, Fig. 3-1 is a kind of funnel. The horn part of the funnel is what we would call the base or the ground of being of the child as he is a very young person—all the curiosity which resides there

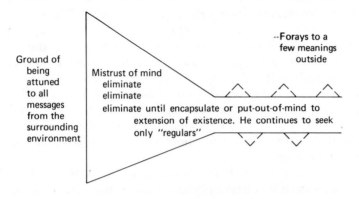

Fig. 3-1. Funneling the approach to meanings.

—the questions and the possibilities for inquiry which are very evident and have not been interfered with. But as the child proceeds through the school his ground of being relative to the seeking of knowledge becomes narrowed. The system or its arrangements are responsible for narrowing the inquiry to a very focal confinement.

The system operates under several assumptions. One of these is that it is better to learn a small amount well than to tackle many things and learn very little about anything. Another assumption is that the minds of children can take only a little at a time. An assumption which is quite prevalent among those who are within the closed system is that an individual's involvement with an extensive domain of meanings tends to confuse him. Still another assumption is that the route to knowledge has been pretty well settled; the arrangements are established together with the content and the direction to be taken relative to achievement. There are still more assumptions more or less unexamined which operate in this funneling approach, but enough have been indicated to describe the operant conditions of the system.

Several elements suggest the thinking in the funneling approach to meanings. There exists, first of all, a mistrust of the mind of the child. The ability of children is underestimated. The child's domain of experiences is not used as clues in their raw state. Immediately as the adult encounters the child, he begins to curtail the child's original domain—

to select out for him what experiences he should have. The child's mind is thus narrowed to conform to the regularity of adult thinking. Another factor that seems apparent in the thinking in this approach is the adult's lack of awareness to the messages which the child has received in his observations previous to the interference of schooling. The closed system has in effect suppressed the receptors of the many media prevalent in the environment. This suppression was experienced by the adult a long time ago. Now he feels he must rise to his responsibility, which requires that he take the child through the same route. In this responsibility the adult has long ceased even to think of behaving with ideas himself in such a way that new meanings may come to him. Instead, all of his behavior is transferred to the child—and in terms of the direction already settled for the child. The whole development is one of narrowing and deprecating the mind.

It will be noted that there are occasional forays suggesting that there is an extension to relationships of meanings that cannot be encompassed in the focused arrangement of the funnel. Examples of forays are field trips and other activities which are prepared for children. These forays, however, always return to the funnel. They are not intended to form new understandings, new points of inquiry, new knowledge, new relationships of meanings or the extension of realities of one's being because they are always pulled back into the funneled arrangement. The system of funneling is developed on the belief that the stretching into relationships in the pursuit of meanings removes anchorage. It also represents an entrapped condition based on "closed" thinking relative to anchor points of meaning. The location places for meanings which existed at the base or starting point have been diminished. Curiosity is reduced, inquiry is narrowed, the direction is settled, the individual is devalued.

The process of funneling characteristic of the closed system of inquiry represents a mistrust of the mind. The condition is one of gradual elimination of the ingredients of curiosity residing in the original experiential domain of the child—the elements of wonderment, awe, the magnificence of the things that can be felt—in short, the real. Funneling tends to reduce the experiential imagery of the self—the medium by which the child approaches integrity with his environment. The result is one of capsulation of experiences and has the effect of putting the child out-of-mind to himself. Any efforts to move out of the regular are designed to produce other "regulars" which resemble those which have been funneled.

The funneling condition produces alienation in the child by moving him away from and out of his experiential domain. Thus his ground for developing his mind has been obscured. The alienation becomes accentuated as he disavows himself as a creature in favor of being someone else.

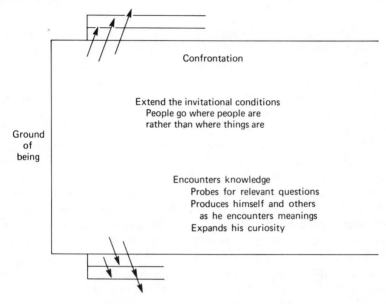

Fig. 3-2. Expanding the approach to meaning.

Figure 3-2 suggests that all arrangements for education should contain those conditions which will expand rather than narrowly focus realities or learnings. Note that the base is the same size as the one with the funnel. In other words, the child began with the same base as in Fig. 3-1. Now as he moves into the years of schooling and progresses through its continuum, new doors open up, and his relationships and meanings are expanded rather than narrowed. The horizontal lines indicate a stabilization of meanings, stabilization of understandings—but never to the point where the ground of being or location places for meanings become narrower than the original base. Meanings are constantly being extended and broadened so that the doors are open to new areas of inquiry. As a person progresses through the school, he becomes broadened in his view of the world, in his manner of relating to content and to meanings; he penetrates deeply into the vast areas of knowledge with great excitement and curiosity. His curiosity at all times is expanded instead of narrowed. The child's location places for knowledge are constantly multiplying. At the same time anchor points are maintained. We will regard here the development of contact points for critical appraisal of all values through the content. In these conditions what is important would be portrayed, as well as that which is *verbalized* as having high estimation. There would be a representative portrayal of what different people hold important. We would relate this to history, to social studies, to world events, and to all other areas of inquiry.

In the open system suggested by Fig. 3-2 we would approach knowledge with an attitude of inquiry, wonderment, search, and the extension of the mind toward extracting meanings from other minds. We would relate genuinely to all phenomena which are representative of learning and the attainment of knowledge. We would try to determine and expand location places for meanings. All media would be in reach for observational inquiry. The teacher as first behaver would extend his domain of observation and increasingly open himself to new messages. All knowledge would be brought into the purview of the child in terms of how he defined the world and himself in it. In promoting the openness toward reality we would try to develop those conditions which provide a scholarly occupation with location places for meanings so that they will become "charged" areas for a turn to knowledge. The special here then becomes the regular which is quite different from the "Closed" where all are approached through the predetermined regular.

In the "open" approach we would provide the conditions for an expanding field of contact points with knowledge and learning. Behavior would be accepted as existent now—not *to become* later. Becoming and being could be conceived as a unity. In this connection the homeostasis theory or drive reduction, which has occupied a prominent place in the thinking about learning in the past, would not be accepted as adequate. We would reconsider the concept of competence. We would draw wisdom from the play of contented children where confidence is now present—behaving now with self-accentuating stimuli. Only the viscerogenic needs are satisfied by satiation. Neurogenic needs are gratified by stimulation. This suggests the needs for novelty, excitement, and an opportunity to deal with the problematic. Interests require elements of unfamiliarity of something still to be found and learning still to be done. A major condition for the exploration of our alternatives in a task is the optimal level of uncertainty. Curiosity is a response to uncertainty and ambiguity.

When we propose to investigate a chosen subject or idea we may be in large part ignorant relative to it. What knowledge we have is just a nibbling at its edges. We do not really *know* what further facts to look for, what facts will tell a significant story of the subject in hand. We can only guess, and proceed to inquire relative to our guesses—all the while trying to ascertain why and how we arrived at our guesses. We will thus take care that we are not trapped by becoming "settled" on initial guesses.

Since in the explosion of knowledge of subject-matter "coverage" is meaningless and obsolete one needs to relate his ingenuity to a transformation in the approach to meanings. It will then be necessary to locate the "key" questions and structures which provide the connections to knowledge and inquiry. We will need always to look for an economy of time in assessing returns for our investment in knowledge. We must try to ascertain only the "circularities" or the major elements of content surrounding the key questions. The "circularities" would provide the connections by which the selective avenues to meanings would be opened.

In formulating a sense of openness toward expanded realities, it is important to ascertain the extent of vacuousness of one's environment. This means that the one who would seek the authentic would try to locate the real "poverty pockets" relative to self-actualization. He would relate himself to the task of ascertaining the extent of those factors that demean and deprecate human dignity and fulfillment, and to locate the elements that elevate human realization. He would try to assess the nature of his behavior with media. He would inquire into the relationship of the media to man's fulfillment for greater existence. He would attempt to relate to the media so that he will become aware of the factors which contribute and those which restrict a definition and redefinition of one's sense of being. This means more than assignments and their completion. It means the impact of waiting and confrontative reflection to ascertain the nature of one's behavior in the elements of vacuity. In this connection, the conditions might warrant a retreat to recapture thought. It may warrant a confrontation center for the production of lucidity as to one's behavior. Here also individuals would try to examine the values between the practical, the realistic, and the real, and to locate the vacuities they have harbored with respect to them.

In furthering existential reality the teachers would need to be the first behavers in ascertaining the extent of their "out-of-awareness" relative to what the system does. When the elements which tend to keep people in a state of "out-of-awareness" to extended realities are detected, one is in a position to break out with responsibility. Then we will work with those elements of a system in which one does not have to compromise the principles of learning. Organization and a certain amount of ordering is always needed—records, grades, carefully developed but flexible lesson plans, and other arrangements. A responsible teacher, one who defines his existence in terms of knowledge which encompasses and overreaches any arrangement, breaks out on the big ideas. It is important to become increasingly aware that the pursuit of wisdom requires more than neat lesson plans and more than "core" or unified studies or any other predesignated patterns for teaching procedures. This awareness will present the substance for one's theories for teaching.

The individual who would seek the authentic would relate to others by ascending to an awareness of their messages and meanings. This is in striking contrast with the condescending relationship of individual to individual characterised by the closed system. Relating to children is not a process of descending to their level but of *ascending* in order to enter into their sphere of awareness. In this approach it is important to examine first how one relates to knowledge while at the same time being receptive to the messages that suggest how individual children relate to knowledge—how they define the world to themselves. It is important in this connection to keep in mind that apparent behavior is not necessarily a true index of how a child relates to meanings or, for that matter, how he relates to the teacher. His apparent behavior may be role behavior and may not at all be a clue to "how it seems to him."

Again, it should be emphasized that in order for one individual to enter into an awareness of another, he must provide a condition of liberation from role behavior. This he may do by a dialogic ascension in which he himself is a behaver who seeks an authentic relationship. He perhaps should open for himself multiple routes of inquiry so that he can locate himself. He needs to know who *he* is. The true self may be located lineally but from a mosaic of media. Through the mosaic the individual can begin to detect and transform the messages of his existence. Even as he is first behaving, he is producing himself and inviting children to help produce himself. Thus he is contributing to a real condition of liberation toward the pursuit of knowledge.

Finally, in the approach to the authentic, one should rejoice without retiring if children and other individuals advance to meanings beyond his realm of understanding. Greatness in teaching is approached when pupils go beyond the teacher. A condition for the elevation for all is a competition for ideas in which a depreciation of human dignity is absent. Face-saving is not needed. That individual who promotes the level of inquiry of others beyond himself will have achieved a greatness, indeed, that should be envied.

SELECTED READINGS

Algren, Nelson. *Nelson Algren's Own Book of Lonesome Monsters.* New York: Random House, 1962.

Combs, Arthur W. (ed.). *Perceiving—Behaving—Becoming.* Washington, D.C.: Association of Supervision and Curriculum Development, NEA, 1962.

Kessen, William. *The Child.* New York: Wiley, 1965, pp. 76-113.

Klopf, Gordon J., and William A. Hohman (eds.). *Perspectives on Learning.*

New York: Mental Health Materials Center, Inc., pp. 1-73.

Maslow, Abraham H. (ed.). *New Knowledge in Human Values.* Foreword by Pitirim A. Sorokin. New York: Harper, 1959, pp. 3-13, 65-75, 107-137, 151-189.

Rosenthal, Robert, and Lenore F. Jacobsen. *Pygmalion in the Classroom.* New York: Holt, 1968, p. 182.

chapter 4

On Adventures with Learners

In a previous chapter an attempt was made to pursue the question of the development of extended realities of individuals without reference to any particular group in the educational continuum. The discussion addressed itself to some extent to "the realistic," the daily occupation with tasks which seem to be necessary in living with the conditions that order an individual's existence. Much of the discussion, however, dealt with some possible "breakthroughs" in this existence so that the individual might find a sense of awareness to meanings suggesting an extension beyond the regular order of things.

It is the purpose of this chapter to propose, discuss, and delineate some facts and conditions that will give direction to the development of extended realities with learners. An attempt will be made to provide some workable theories, principles, and suggested practices relative to the commitment.

In the approach to the problem of developing extended realities, one should give due credit to the work of many teachers who are making great efforts in this direction. Much of what will be suggested is not necessarily new. Many people in education are doing a good deal in promoting extended realities with learners. Nothing in the ensuing pages is intended as a grand design to supplant what is going on in great teaching.

Basic to the plans needed to extend realities with children is the assumption that regular programs are in operation for the development of skills in reading, language and other areas. In the overall approach to learning these are essential in any effort to extend the meanings for learners. Although the regular reading and other programs are designed for developmental purposes, they can constitute an important phase in the ground of meanings toward extended realities. They can become some of the media which give messages for extended meanings.

OCCUPATION WITH SKILLS EXTENDS INTO MANY MEDIA AND RELATIONSHIPS

As one observes children it soon becomes apparent that they are very much occupied with skills of all types. It is further apparent that the skills are both physical and verbal with no sharp lines of distinction made between the skills. Children tend to "locate" themselves with both physical and verbal skills simultaneously. For example, as pre-school children play with the dollhouse they speak of being "inside" or "outside." "Where can you find Jane?" asks one child, and the other responds with any number of locations, depending on where Jane is. To extend the reality the teacher may suggest the location of each or all of the children as being in the classroom, being in the school, going outside for certain games, running from this place to where Bill is, and so on. As children talk and read, their thoughts might drift to other places, such as where they go after school, where they find themselves when food is served, and where they go for the night. All the time they are locating themselves with realities which surround them in their roles with school and family and other places of association. The teachers as first behavers are doing the same relative to their own inquiries.

As children locate themselves with different learning situations the teacher in his involvement with them might note the concepts that appear to evolve from their experiences. One generalization children might make is that they can tell where they might be at certain times of the day without actually going there. Another development is that if in describing all the places they might visit in a day they actually had to travel to them, they would be all tired out. Furthermore, it would take much time. Then it is, perhaps, more fun to talk about the places—to use words and sentences which will describe the places and tell what was done. Besides, this would give more time to play with objects and things in the classroom. The use of words in conversation has made this possible. Isn't it astounding to be able to do so many things with words without using our legs, arms, and so on? This fact could in all probability be arrived at by the children as they move into extended plans with the realities that surround them.

It should become clear as one thinks about the experiences of children—their life space and daily habitude, that their realities are extended by the provision for greater curiosity about their surroundings, the strange and interesting phenomena with which they relate day after day. The reference to children's experiences should always be considered in association with thinking. It is the behavior responsibility of the teacher to relate himself to the phenomena and to note what happens to him. At the same time, he will portray features of the phenomena as he views them, and note how children relate to them. He will have gained some degree of cognizance as to how children relate to different experiences in their daily environment. Since ours is a verbal as well as physical culture, a sizable segment of the environment takes the form of books of all kinds. Besides books, there are all kinds of objects in the classroom-encountered environment of the children—toys of various types, objects of a variety of shapes and forms, boxes of various weights and contents, "streamers" with sentences related to times and places, and many types of designs and pictures. The encounters in the environment would extend into other media with which the child is continuously occupied.

Learning experiences extend beyond any single medium. One of the most valued priorities of the open system of inquiry is the trust of the mind. Any first behavior of individuals would be associated with this phenomenon. The most important encounter toward the development of meanings is with minds in the immediate setting. A teacher, as a first behaver, would regard as the richest resources the minds of other individuals. The encounter of one mind with another should be more productive than that with books, objects, and other inanimate resources. This encounter becomes central to the development of meanings. In the closed system there appears to be a mistrust of the mind. Teachers and children place first priority on the book, the workbook, the blackboard, articles, objects, and other paraphernalia. This idea is associated with the concept that minds are "containers" which need to be "filled."

As suggested above, perhaps the first priority in the open system is behavior which is associated with the trust of the mind. Thinking is valued above everything else. Accordingly, the conditions of behavior which are central are those through which individuals accentuate each other's thinking. From this derives the confrontation between minds in which one mind helps produce the other. With this confrontation there arises a condition of relating to many minds in order to develop one's own mind. As this continues, the capacity of the mind is expanded for ever greater extraction of meanings from other minds.

The condition of retrieval between minds has the added tendency of the development of respect of one individual for another. Also, in this connection there should arise a true confrontation between individuals as to the concerns which each one has relative to the other's manner of existence. Thus there comes about a real dialogue expressive of human quality and the expansion of the conditions for the appreciation and advancement of the dignity of individuals. The human values of people then come into play, which in turn accentuate deeper concern about man's relationship to man.

Although highest priority resides in the trust of the mind, the importance of books and other media is by no means diminished. In fact, books take on greater importance because books are a result of the action of minds. Greater trust of the mind then will result in greater books and other media. As minds confront one another they become ever more attuned to the messages derived through observations of the nature of the media and the phenomena surrounding them.

Some of the experiences with which children obviously would be engaged are those associated with books of all sorts. No doubt, the teacher would read to the children from these books with a view to help them establish some identity with the experiences they describe. Furthermore, the children would view the medium of television for contact with experiences. As the children would regard again their experiences in locating themselves in different places they would now find that other children were associated with these same experiences as clearly indicated in the books, pictures, and other media. At times, too, they would decide that their own experiences were more extended and occupied many more locations than those represented in reading books, viewing television, and making conversation contacts with others. In fact, they would probably discover that their life space represented much greater dimensions than that indicated in the readings and other media encountered.

The medium of television is perhaps, the most extensive domain of experience encountered by children. The experiences here are simultaneous and all-encompassing of the child's senses. As McLuhan[1] has stated in reference to television, *the medium is the message.* He suggests that sequence yields to the simultaneous in many areas of content. Rather than approaching learning by a step-by-step procedure there is instant total awareness of the whole. He suggests also that the message is actually more than the content in the electronic age. In television children have finally encountered a medium which invites total involvement. To be involved is always central to a child's desire. Actually, everyone craves involvement in varying degrees. The literate culture which has more or less been absorbed by the closed system guards against too much involvement for obvious reasons. Books are lineal, in that they enforce the pursuit of meanings in terms of short sequences—a little-at-a-time effect—the "walk-before-you-run" admonition.

The child has been shifted from the world of sequence and con-

[1]Marshall McLuhan, *Understanding Media* (New York: New American Library, 1964), p. 28.

nections into the world of configuration and structure. In the electronic environment the whole sensory structure of the child is involved. While the child is in this condition of involvement he must feel the encounter with school procedures somewhat strange, especially since the school personnel who are "children of the lineal culture" fail to respond to the electronic culture which comes as feedback to the classroom via the children. The feedback is probably viewed by the school people as strange behavior quite foreign to their accustomed manner of relating to children. The behavior may do something to the school personnel but they are not prepared to determine what it is. The only points of identification are, perhaps, elements of unresolvable conflict with what has been the mode of operation. The behavior exhibited by those who are involved with the electronic world does not seem to resemble the requirements that have become more or less routine in the arrangements of the closed system. McLuhan,[2] in emphasizing that the individual hears and touches as well as sees, suggests a real contradiction in our verbalization that education should bring meanings to individuals and our actual practices when he says, "It is in our IQ testing that we have produced the greatest flood of misbegotten standards. Unaware of our typographic cultural bias, our testers assume that uniform and continuous habits are a sign of intelligence, thus eliminating the ear man and the tactile man." The proponents of the standards may fit the discussion that McLuhan refers to when he says, "For the man in a literate and homogenized society ceases to be sensitive to the diverse and discontinuous life of forms."[3]

The statements by McLuhan seem to suggest much more than is encountered in many television programs. It appears that he would be the first to deny that television should be used to imitate a regularized form of presentation. He would, on the contrary, emphasize an openness to the infiltration of meanings quite removed from the settled arrangements of the IQ type of intelligence proponents. Furthermore, he would not contend that the development of a sensitivity to "the diverse and discontinuous life of forms" would be encountered only in television. The fact remains, however, that television has become the medium of liberation which allows this diversity and discontinuity to happen.

The presentation which suggests diversity and discontinuity does not have to be confined to television. To illustrate this, one has but to take a walk through a woods or along a country road. All kinds of diverse and discontinuous facts become apparent as one listens, touches, hears,

[2] *Ibid.*, pp. 31-32.
[3] *Ibid.*, p. 33.

and thinks. The writer had the good fortune to take such walks with a father and his small son. Although many observations occurred through seeing, the father made it a point to listen to the woods and the life in it. There were the songs and calls of many birds. Some of the birds responded to his imitations of their songs. There were the sounds of the wind whistling through the tops of the pine trees. Some distance away the water of a lake was lapping against the rocks. Some homes of animals were sighted and touched. The question of how the animals made their homes so as to give comfort to them was gone into. The father, who has some knowledge of birds and their habitat, sighted one that was not supposed to be in the particular region where the walks were taken. He explained that the life of forms is not necessarily continuous.

In the types of experiences encountered in these walks there was no lack of messages. They bombarded the participants from all angles. Nor was there any apparent and constricting sequence. The messages were simultaneous. The imaginative flow of conversation which occurred both during the walks and following them hardly resembled a book. There was a real configuration of meanings. No real stopping and starting places encumbered the occupation with the messages. The parties to the walk were involved in the messages with their whole sensorium. There were no central tie-ins such as is found in many books, but there was a mosaic of meanings which invited further probing for ideas. There was spontaneity in the response which involved sound, tactility, sight, mind, and heart. The electronic effect pervaded the responses to the experiences. It was, indeed, a great show with the medium as the message.

The spontaneity associated with an experience should prevail over and above all available media. There is a great temptation on the part of educators to suggest that after an experience such as has just been described, books take on more meaning to children. This, of course, may be obvious. To gear the experience for this purpose, however, may almost constitute a deterioration of a human by the very act of manipulating him into the ordered arrangement. The experience should stand by itself. It should not be relegated to the standards of the usual sequential arrangements of books. If a book should come out of this experience (and it very well could), the experience should stand preeminent without embellishment to produce a lineality effect. The experience must exist by itself with all its electronic effects. Perhaps it should be an "electronic book." The child must stand above the book. Never should he become subservient to it. This may be illustrated by the way a young child views a book. He turns several pages at a time to relate the book to his encounters with meanings. There is usually a great temptation for the adult to laboriously take the child through the book page by page.

This may be a mistake, often manifested by the child jumping from the lap of the adult to go to other things. He is expressing boredom because he is being made subservient to the pages. He has a sense of spontaneity. He wants to be involved with the wonderment which he has encountered in the electronic environment. In fact, he might even at this young age produce a better book than the one he is required to peruse.

The writer himself can be accused of somehow submitting to the habit of the priority of the "book" in working with children. It is, indeed, difficult to shed the ways of the culture and the arrangements of the systems. It is hoped that the reader of the ideas presented here should get into real dialogue with the writer and, in fact, go beyond him in developing spontaneity in experiences with children. The writer would, indeed, rejoice if he had a small part in making this happen. Perhaps one must put himself into question and thereby approach the predicament of existence, which condition will enable him to define himself into a state of expanded being.

When the experiences of these children are in advance of the experiences of children in the books, extended realities become apparent. The contact points with surrounding phenomena can then be multiplied in various ways. For example, the children could be pursuing the *why* of their locations in different places during their daily life pattern. In fact, there is no special reason why this discourse has been concerned with the *where* of children. Furthermore, there is no special sequence which would need to be considered in venturing with children into the *where, why, when,* and *how much* of their own experiences as well as those encountered by other children in the books. The location of children relative to their experiences along with the reasons for these could be integrated with the times of the experiences as well as the number of them.

It should be emphasized that their experiences will locate them with all kinds of people, many of whom may have needs and problems which are different from theirs. In pursuing with intensive concern these locations in terms of *why, where,* and *how much*, children would become aware of the nature of living of different humans and the means through which they carry on their existence. As children read, discuss, and relate to the various messages, the whole question of poverty and affluence which surrounds their existence comes into their purview. Values associated with their concerns about the poor, the rich, care, love, and human dignity will become real in their acts of inquiry. These concerns will become central to the content which will be encountered in their pursuit of meanings. These would all be part of the same experiences toward greater existence for them.

The possibilities for extended realities indicated in the above discussion are so extensive that it is difficult to know where one should begin. It would seem very probable that with teacher and pupil behavior in the experiential environment, opportunities for countless points of identification for children would develop. As a result, both teacher and pupils would find themselves moving beyond the limits of the readings. Some of the experiences in which children might engage would demand more than the readings to encompass expanded meanings. As children read and talk about "Jane"—what she is doing and thinking—they would be fashioning new media and symbolization which would take them to many location places that provide meaning reception. To do this they would literally have to write new books and enter into an encounter with each other's minds for the extension of thought.

Many location places for meanings could be developed in connection with experiences in the need and use of language. One can, for example, remain seated in a chair yet be in many places in the mind. All kinds of movement, then, can be represented through the use of words and sentences. Then too, we can develop an awareness of staying in one place and reading about experiences happening to people all over the world. Also, as children are playing with toys or games they will be chattering continuously, creating most of their pleasure in this manner. In most games and in most of the play engaged in by children, use of language becomes a major aspect of their activities. As children grow into an awareness of the importance of language in extending their feelings they extend themselves into a greater existence with it. Physical play and verbal play become a unity. John Dewey frequently emphasized not only this type of unity but also the unity between work and play. Work could be defined as an extended occupation with one's curiosity, which, in reality, is play. It can hardly be denied that language is integrally wound up with curiosity. It follows too that as curiosity is expanded, words become more valuable, taking on expanded meanings.

It can be generalized that words are symbols of the phenomena surrounding one and make possible an experiencing of time and place which one is incapable of enjoying physically. Words as symbols enable us to play with time and place without locomotion. Through the symbolism provided by reading and conversation, we experience not only what has happened in other times and places, but what is happening today. Reading can be started as soon as a child can engage in extensive play. As he plays with toys he will play with letters and words. Certainly he will be thoughtfully as well as playfully involved with pictures. As he becomes involved with words, letters, sentences, and pictures he will continuously discover why this occupation will tend to further his purposes and give him exciting meanings.

In this discourse, reading and the need and use of language are discussed interchangeably. Again, it should be emphasized that the most important attitude of the behavers should relate to the trust of the mind. This should hold priority over books, so-called enrichment materials, and other media. Thus reading is not confined to the perusal of the printed page. Rather it is conversation, play, story telling, story invention, and minds encountering each other through listening, response, and dialogue. It can truly be said that if the priority of the trust of mind were a continuous condition in school, books and other media would be improved most spectacularly over those now in existence. Almost any group of children (their minds trusted) in conversation together could develop the discourse which would carry vitality in content and meanings which might far surpass that found in many books and materials.

Children begin to recognize rather early that play and work are a part of the daily routine—the *stuff* which is a part of growing up. They will further recognize that with this growing up, many symbols are involved—numbers, the spoken word, the written word, and others not only to give meaning to immediate reality but also to extended realities. In short, children will become ever more conversant and facile with the use of the symbols to extend their existence. In this connection, through their expanded structuring of the encountered environment, children will become associated with another conceptual relationship with the symbols—that of thinking. This can develop by treating the encounter with symbols more than as a perusal. Rather, the symbols encountered evoke a response. This will be more or less simple and natural in the type of involvement experienced with the spoken word in conversation. Thinking here will become a going concern. If, however, language development is approached too sharply in connection with a "language series," with workbooks and formal aids, the experience will be one in which most of the messages in the child's environment will not be encountered. Thus a real limiting condition to the use of language in thinking may become apparent. This fact should receive very serious consideration in the efforts to facilitate the spoken word and sentence in thinking. It would seem advisable, therefore, in the efforts to facilitate thinking that the program development tasks include content which will evoke at least as much response in kind as is affirmed. It follows that the development of language skills through the use of language-series materials and aids may suffer in that not much response in thinking outside of artificial activities has been envisioned in this form of program. To develop extended realities demands conditions which permit free flow of response with the content. Since the content is a result of mind, the child needs to be in conversation with it.

As a child begins to read, he is thinking all the time about more than is involved in the act of reading. He is reacting in such a way as to evoke hundreds of responses which are not directly associated with the lines on the page of the book. As a child peruses the content of a reading series, the least that should be done to give play to his responses is to help him develop response experiences to his reading. These he may record in his own way in a book of his own creation. This would probably be much more helpful to him than a workbook. Here he would devise his own book which would contain his responsive writing, his pictures, and other points he would like to talk about. The teacher, rather than having so many reading sessions from the regular reading series, would do well to devote some sessions during a week to a discussion and perusal of the response books of the children. This most necessary phase of the reading and language program should certainly promote some authentic meanings. Besides this, the responses could well constitute a redevelopment of the reading content as presented by the publishers.

In any type of reading program much attention should be given to the matter of *thinking out loud.* This is implied in the discussion above. Of course, much of this is done by some teachers. Mostly, however, it is treated as a sort of side issue. Rather, it should be in the main stream of the reading program. What is more important, this practice should not only be encouraged during reading sessions but should become an important phase of each child's silent reading. In this connection, it would be well to suggest to children to have with them some note pads where, while reading a book, they could from time to time enter their *thinking out loud* notes. This could be referred to as *My Thinking Out Loud* book. Teachers would do well not only to encourage this practice but to devote periodic sessions to a discussion and reading of this content if the children wish to divulge this phase of their thinking. One can almost be assured of their desire to share this type of thinking. The encouragement of children to respond in this manner would be a most significant step in the development of extended realities. Not only would skills and inquiry be developed, but more concerted dispositions toward humanization through reading would emerge.

As emphasized in the previous sections, different opportunities for responses on the part of children through reading and language experiences should do much to extend their realities and develop positive attitudes toward learning and inquiry. Furthermore, the practices associated with the opportunities would extend the curiosity of children relative to new and related meanings. Since the curiosity of individual children would be expanded, there would follow a compulsive need on their part to "stretch out" in the acquisition of skills so that fulfillment of curiosity and concern may be enhanced. Meanwhile the teacher would be noting how the individual children approached this "stretching out" condition and would continuously invoke the efforts of children to provide the substance and media in terms of how the children related to knowledge. In this connection, too, the clues for the development of expanded content would be clearly indicated. There would be a ready-made condition for curriculum development, and this would be participated in by staff and children.

The development of conceptual relationships by thinking through the areas of reading and language has been discussed. In a former section the matter of a response workbook was suggested relative to reading. This was aimed at giving free flow to the responses which children might have as they read the *series* materials and other books. This condition could also be developed with respect to language activities. *Thinking out loud* responses were recommended. At the same time, responses should be encouraged by suggesting that children might talk much without using the vocal organs such as the mouth. Furthermore, they can hear much without the presence of sound. This might be considered an initiation of the practice of thinking as it is carried on by individuals in the pursuit and development of extended meanings or ideas. This thinking could be recorded by children in many different ways. One way would be by drawing pictures. Another way would be to "tell it to Jim's group." If the child was sufficiently conversant with a writing vocabulary to encompass his responses he could either write them or choose word cards in stating his ideas. Still another and rather exciting way would be to tell his ideas to a tape recorder. Other children might do this too and then exchange the records to share their thinking. Certainly, these exchanges and experiences would tend to extend the realities of children and advance their existence with meanings to a degree that might establish a broadening threshold of skills and values in the approach to areas of inquiry.

Openness to experience invites and accentuates differences. The discourse relative to reading and language up to this point hardly suggests a uniform or smooth development. As one reads this, no doubt many questions may arise as to individual learners and their abilities to do what has been suggested. Children, of course, differ from one to another. There are differences in home conditions, in peer relationships, in environmental opportunities. Some have had more opportunities than others. Some have by some reason been favored with more ability, energy, and so on. Some have had more media within reach or have encountered messages through much observation. As a result the progress of different children through the program will be varied. Some will respond quickly to the invitational clues of the learning environment. Others will have difficulties. Some will encounter many frustrations. Still others will find themselves at a standstill. Some specific questions which may arise are in the order of the following. Aren't the expectations too ideal? Don't children have to learn to read according to a basic vocabulary as designed in any one of the reading series before they can do all the things suggested? Wouldn't the inclusion of all children in this type of program lead to complete defeat and frustration on the part of those who are not able to go along?

The above, of course, are all-important issues and questions that must be dealt with. The purpose of the suggestions and possible programs indicated is to respond to all types of children. Some of the children will learn to read quite readily and will progress even faster than anyone has anticipated. Others will have some difficulty and will need considerable help and guidance. With a degree of guidance they will be able to help themselves. Perhaps the imaginative teacher will establish some conversation "clinics" with help from other children and himself whereby these children will be able to ascertain their "stoppage places" and to start from there. Still others have veritably stopped dead in their tracks. For these, special conversation "clinics" can be developed where they will converse with the teacher relative to the nature of their "stoppage places'" and other predicaments. It should be understood that this "clinic" and the one mentioned previously are not designed to "bring children up to grade level" nor to bring about like patterns in the pursuit of materials for the acquisition of skills as such. Rather, the purpose of the clinics is to help the teacher to help himself and the individual child in making responses to, and deriving messages from, the learning environment. A very important aspect of the clinic sessions is for the teacher to gain some conception as to how each child relates to things around him and then help him use some simple means to extend this relationship. At the same time the teacher will be relating to things around him and extending his area of meanings. The clinics would provide the conditions for many confrontations with ideas as among the children and the teacher and to devise ways in the form of developing pictures, using words and sentences, and other means of portrayal in their response to the ideas. The teacher would be doing likewise in his world of responses.

The confrontation between the children which may be extended to the teacher could be a sort of "self-discovery" occasion relative to possible deficiencies which they have encountered. The teacher would be involved with a self-discovery effort to ascertain certain deficiencies to his being. Children may try to discover answers as to what "stops them" or "what stands in the way" relative to the fulfillment of tasks they have begun. They may try to determine the interferences that occur most frequently when they are reading or doing their language work and trying to develop their responses. The deficiencies could relate to "thought stoppage," that is, the ascertaining of the points at which their minds seemed to give no service. They could attempt to respond to such questions as: When does my thinking seem to stop? When does thinking *not* tell me? It may be that they are trying to think too much and react too much before they have read and observed enough. Perhaps their responses would be much different if they read further in the book or read in a related or companion book. Perhaps they could have helped themselves by talking with the teacher or some of the other pupils before they reacted to a reading or language exercise. In other words, *clinics* (or whatever else they may be called—consultation centers, inquiry stations, or just reading tables) will become more than "help" places. Rather, they may constitute the areas where the real programs are developed, where curiosity is expanded, and where creativity receives greatest fulfillment. These areas or centers should be such a major part of the program that all the children in a classroom will at different times be involved with them.

The fact that the clinics or centers should be in the mainstream of any instructional program does not preclude their functioning as "trouble location" places relative to skills. As suggested above, questions relative to stoppage places and interferences to successful pursuit of meanings would be confronted. The centers become self-discovery locations as well as regular instruction and development areas to further inquiry. They would certainly constitute most fruitful areas in the development of extended realities.

Children's experiences include many confrontations with meanings. Up to this point the discussion relative to the development of skills and extended realities has dealt mainly with the development of expanded meanings through reading and language and other media. As previously indicated, the word *skills* is somewhat of a misnomer, since the questions of attitudes and values are also involved. Furthermore, the practice of skill development separate from the pursuit of meanings for appreciation, enjoyment, and retrieval of mind should be disavowed. It would indeed be difficult to separate skill development from the pursuit of ideas toward greater existence in all its dimensions. At this point, instead of following a natural tendency to indicate how children relate to social studies, we will consider their possible occupation with various objects in the learning environment.

Perhaps the most prevalent ventures with learners would be approached in their occupation with play. Children come to know much about the environment through their play activities. Actually, the ways of people as they live and move in the environment are relived by children through play. Many years ago Froebel[4] in his writings about the education of man expressed himself most emphatically relative to the importance of play by children and older people.

> Play is the purest, most spiritual activity of man at this state [childhood] and, at the same time, typical of human life as a whole—of the inner hidden natural life in man and all things. It gives, therefore, joy, freedom, contentment, inner and outer rest, peace with the world. It holds the sources of all that is good. A child that plays thoroughly, with self-active determination, perseveringly until physical fatigue forbids, will surely be a thorough, determined man, capable of self-sacrifice for the promotion of the welfare of himself and others.

Perhaps some of the most intriguing media for meanings that children can encounter in play are toys. Toys might be thought of as play objects which are representative of the items in the child's culture. Toys suggest movement, life, manipulative features, mechanistic design, and to a degree man's conquest of nature. Children relish toys because it makes them a part of the surrounding realism in terms of their ability to exercise some form of control. By means of the toys children relate to movement, the technology, the structure of mechanisms, and, in the case of dolls and other forms of caricatures of human beings, how life is interesting and is to be cared for. The cherished institutions of a culture such as home and family, modes of making a living, church, school, and defenses are represented in toys. It would seem that the structure of the conditions for learning to include toys would add a vital avenue toward extended realities and meanings for greater existence for children.

As children bring their toys to school or contemplate them at home, they will, with some amount of structuring, note likenesses and differences among the toys. There will be girl toys, boy toys, animal toys, toys that move by means of electric motors, toys that move by spring mechanisms, and those that have to be moved by hand. All types of classifications can be made of the different toys in terms of what they represent in mechanical construction, simulation of activities of people, and new dimensions of generative power. Other types of examination of the toys could be in terms of physical properties, tools used in manufacturing (whether construction was by hand or machine), and what determines value in terms of expense. In connection with these analyses and classifications, all types of discussion and confrontations with extended ideas should arise. For example, in considering the classification of self-generative power toys, some children may wish to inquire into

---

[4]Friedrich Froebel, *The Education of Man* (New York: Appleton, 1901), p. 55.

the operation of cars and trucks. They may discuss such topics as different types of gears, transmissions, clutches, compression, hydraulics in connection with brakes, and any number of other items. In discussing gears, children might examine the power-driven toys to see whether gears are a part of the mechanism. A closer examination may reveal the different sizes of gears and what effect this has on locomotion of a vehicle. Some of the more insightful children may recognize an elementary principle about gear ratios. For example, they may notice that when a large-sized gear works with a small-sized gear, the smaller gear moves faster than the larger one. Thus the speed of a toy or large vehicle would be determined by the location of the gears with respect to axles of the vehicle. In terms of the principle of gear ratios, some children could make a transfer in thinking relative to slow- and fast-moving vehicles. This thinking might be stretched into a recognition of the need for both slow and fast vehicles in the work which people do. Questions which might be considered in this connection are the following: When does a car or truck have to move slowly? Why does a car move slowly when starting? What type and sizes of gears are used at low speed? Why does a tractor move slower than a car? What are the types of gears used in a high-speed operation of a car or truck?

The responses to these questions by different children would give important clues as to how they relate to knowledge in terms of the principle indicated. Some would inquire further than the questions suggest. All who gain some concepts about the principles of operation of toys and vehicles would certainly be enroute to extending their ideas about reality.

Before going any further into a discussion of the extension of realities of children through the study of toys it would perhaps be helpful to indicate the rationale involved in the procedures suggested. It should be clear that there is prevalent in these procedures an emphasis on the structure of knowledge. In a sense, the emphasis is in terms of that advocated by Bruner[5] when he states: "Grasping the structure of a subject is understanding it in a way that permits many other things to be related to it meaningfully. To learn structure, in short, is to learn how things are related."

Although the emphasis as advocated by Bruner is related to a subject, it would seem plausible that the idea of structure could be extended over and beyond the time-honored disciplines. The point to be made here specifically is that the structure approached in the study of toys as well as that associated with reading and language previously

[5]Jerome S. Bruner, *The Process of Education* (Cambridge: Harvard U. P., 1961), p. 7.

described is developed quite apart from any established discipline. That does not mean that elements of one or more disciplines may not be involved. What is done here is to proceed into extended relationships with ideas without regard to the limiting conceptions of this or that discipline. The principle of gear ratios would, for example, relate largely to the area of mechanics which is part of a major discipline, physics. As children relate to toys in their various classifications, connections and relationships are established to any number of areas of knowledge such as mathematics, physics, social sciences, locomotion both mechanical and human (body movements), thermodynamics, language, and biological sciences. Perhaps, what is being done here is to structure for knowledge rather than consciously pursuing the structure of knowledge as if it is already established.

In the study of toys it might be helpful to suggest various directions children might make in extending the relationships of ideas. In the study of gears, for example, the teacher might help to structure the ideas resulting from the various confrontations so as to point to an extension of meanings relative to the principle of the use of gears. The teacher as a learner might simulate some mechanism relating to locomotion and invite conversation and open-ended discussion as to the various ways of locomotion and the instrumentation involved. Certainly, the use of gears is involved more or less with one type of locomotion. Through pictures and books children will discover other types of locomotion such as jet propulsion and centrifugal force. Furthermore, there should be developed an "openness to experience" which will invite all types of inquiry into the various forms of locomotion, including those connected with space travel. In fact, the teacher is the first behaver in relating to the question of locomotion. His experience involves a real sense of receptiveness to the ideas of other individuals. Also, it is hoped that some children will extend their thinking to basic questions such as man and his motivations, including his form of locomotion. One of the most interesting "motors" is the human heart, surrounded by a "chassis," an engineering marvel which approaches a high state of perfection. Here one would go into the structure of knowledge relative to the discipline of physiology. Yet within this discipline many sub-disciplines are discerned. Questions that might arise with respect to locomotion and the human body are: Is the heart at the center of man's locomotion? How does the heart compare with a motor? In what way is the mind involved in helping a body move? How is aliveness related to movement? What are the elements which are related to being alive?

As these questions are approached, the whole matter of aliveness as related to heart, mind, and body locomotion could develop as a point of real concern and meaning. Values associated with expressions about the heart, such as "He speaks from the heart," "He loves with his whole heart," may become part of the conversation of children. The whole question of love and its association with aliveness, need, and humanness could be an extension of meaning. The topic of locomotion and that of mind could be generative of larger meanings in connection with matters of concern, love, and decision. Action often suggests locomotion and movement. Hence, as one acts he moves to the places where his concern is or where he can serve another human being. Real neighborliness is often shown when one person goes to help another.

The mind can become an important accompaniment—in fact, the vital factor—in the approach to meanings through the employment of toys. The mind, in the approach to the problems of people, is the instrument of decision for action by the other parts of the body. The decision of the mind as it relates to other minds is based on more than utilitarian considerations. It can have as its base that of love, true concern, regard for need, the elevation of the dignity of man, and may relate to all human beings with a real sense of care and affinity.

Man approaches an intimate behavior with the disciplines through inquiry into phenomena. As children ponder questions such as those discussed above, they may begin to realize that they are related to their surroundings quite differently and more extensively than is suggested by the world of toys. For example, man has to breathe, he needs to sleep, he has to take nourishment, and his body performs many functions to keep him alive and healthy. Man becomes related to air, water, food, sunshine, and many elements incident to these items. He thus is a part of chemistry, has biological connections, and in some ways is related to physics, the social sciences, and perhaps to the quantitative disciplines. Man thus becomes the center of the structure of the disciplines.

To illustrate how man is related to the various disciplines, one might consider air in association with man's behavior. What types of behavior does man exhibit relative to air, and what are the concepts that may emerge in the study of this behavior? A quesion which both pupils and teachers might ask is, What types of impact does air exert on man's behavior that lead him to gain concepts about it? First of all, one has to consider the primary contacts which man makes with air so as to recognize some primary tasks in learning about himself. Air is necessary for life. It goes without saying that when one stops breathing he dies or "expires," or "breathes out." Thus air is a life-giving element. Without air life does not go on. Nor does this apply only to man—it applies equally to animals and plants. In examining the substance of air, therefore, it is important to ascertain its life-giving elements. A primary experiment to explain the principle of air as a life-giving element may be the effort to indicate the listless behavior of an animal in an enclosure from which some air has been withdrawn. Another and perhaps more humane experiment is to try to grow plants in an environment from which air has been removed. Obviously, the plants will not thrive because air is a part of the soil ingredients. Some other phenomena which might be developed with respect to air is the relationship about the need of opening windows, "being cooped up" in a room for some time because of weather elements, and being unable to stay underwater for any length of time without air apparatus.

When one approaches man and his relation to the disciplines the central concern is that they provide the means and conditions for him to extend his existence. In turn, man gives greater life to the disciplines. He expands and enlivens their content. He actually becomes intimate with the disciplines so that he will be in true conversation with them. His mind is in relation to other minds, all of which have had some impact in creating and extending the disciplines which in turn help produce his and other minds. In thinking of air as a life-giving element, it follows that man has developed a discipline of knowledge about the nature of air which is designed to serve him and his fellow-men. As one begins to have dialogue with the question of air, he may find that in his efforts to acquire an affluential existence he has interfered with the life-giving quality of air. He may unwittingly be depreciating the quality of existence of his fellow-men as well as himself through the growing problem of air pollution.

Children in their own behavior and teachers as first behavers should indeed approach the whole question of air pollution and the responsibility of the mind to relate to other minds in real social decision making and action regarding this problem. The motivations which eventuate the condition of air pollution should be gone into with real concern. To what extent is this a result of a condition of dehumanization? What are the values which appear to be inherent in these motivations? Why would individuals reduce the quality of living for themselves and others? It is important, of course, that the scientific facts relative to this condition should be discussed, as well as the social and humanization facts. What are the ingredients of air reduction, for example? The question here obviously becomes more than one about pollution. The matter of values and their relationship to priorities must be intensively considered. Perhaps the priorities have resulted from a lack of trust of minds. Perhaps, the arrangement for production has become so regularized that a condition of congealing has set in which funnels all thinking to a point of out-of-awareness. Again the stoppage places to thinking need to be assessed not only in the experiences in learning but in the experiences that surround us and have given rise to some real interferences to human existence.

There are other characteristics of air which will tend to develop extended realities. One of these facts is that air occupies space and can be stored. It can also be enriched. Deep-sea divers carry storage tanks of air with them. The stored air is, however, measured in terms of amount of usage over a period of time. A deep-sea diver is given a record of the amount of air which is at his disposal and if he exceeds this amount as measured in time, he will suffer serious consequences, even death. For children, therefore, it is important to think of air as fresh and being all around us and freely available. With some children the subject of oxygen might be discussed.

A simple concept that can be developed about air is that it provides shape and form. An example of this is a rubber balloon before it is inflated. As one breathes air into it it takes shape. People at fairs who sell balloons have air as one of their products. Although the balloon sellers have a few balloons on display, when a customer purchases a balloon the seller inflates it for him. One might say in this connection that air takes on economic value since the product which becomes a balloon with air is originally shapeless and useless to the user. Incidentally, balloons are favorite toys for many children. This might be considered as extended reality for children.

Another concept about air is that it occupies space. This is the space in which one lives. Man moves and has his being in air. Actually man is quite literally "floating" in air. Air is all around him—around his body, in his ears, eyes, mouth, and in all parts of his body. In fact, an unusual blast of air to certain parts of his body may cause a degree of pain. How often have we heard one say "I feel a draft" which meant an unusual amount of air going in a certain direction is encountering a certain part of his body. One of the usual experiments found in many textbooks is that of heating the air in a punctured fruit-juice can to drive off the gas, causing the can to collapse. Observations and confrontations relative to this phenomenon would certainly reveal many messages about the nature of air.

In connection with the above concept, one might pursue the idea of air in relation to coldness and heat. Some questions that might develop here are: Why am I cold sometimes? Why do I feel hot sometimes? The obvious answers are the action of molecules. It is difficult, however, to explain molecules to young children in terms of the usual conception of molecules. It may be possible to improvise some image such as small balls knocking against each other. The answers might have something to do with the action of molecules. One might be able to show how molecules behave with temperature. Does the action of molecules have any relationship with our feelings of comfort and discomfort with varying temperatures? The whole question of heating and cooling would extend to the use of furnaces, fans, and air-conditioning installations. What is involved in the behavior of air in heating a house when the temperature is low? What behaviors are introduced into air by cooling devices such as fans and air-conditioning units? What happens to air when we say "It is very humid today"? How does humidity in the air relate to our comfort or discomfort? The discussion on the above question would no doubt lead into the topic of evaporation and its effects on heating and cooling.

There are, of course, many other ways in which man's behavior is related to the phenomenon of air. Some concepts beyond those indicated previously which may be developed are those related to flight and possibly pressure. Simple toy airplanes may be used to demonstrate the use of air in flight. Perhaps the simplest experiments would be the airplanes made out of folded paper. As these are thrust forward, they will glide slowly to the ground. The child will notice the difference between thrusting the folded paper in the shape of an airplane and doing the same with an unfolded sheet of paper. In making the little tests about air as substance, children may wish to develop the media which would indicate impactful meanings about the nature of air. It is always important to invite children to make inferences and generalizations about their observations before many final facts are brought into the setting for learning. If facts which have a finality are brought in too soon, observations which should have been made and which are not in the facts may be missed altogether. Thus the possibilities for real creative imagination may be severely limited.

The approach to the development of concepts about air pressure may be through conditions which portray situations where air is escaping from some enclosure with a hissing sound. An example of this would be the gradual escape of air from a balloon. Another example would be the act of letting air out of a tire. Air pressure can be observed as a truckdriver brings his truck to a standstill. Almost invariably there is a sharp sound of the escape of air from the air brakes. The observations of air pressure become significant as pupils begin to extract messages and meanings from their observations. Such questions as the following might be raised by the children: Why does air make noise as it is released from a tire? Is there more air in a tire than is usually around us wherever we go? How is air pressure useful to people? Does the amount of air in a given space have anything to do with pressure? What types of uses does air have outside of its life-giving qualities? What keeps a can from collapsing when it is not heated? Teachers who are constructively patient to wait for meanings to emerge will bring rewarding experiences to themselves and to children.

In approaching the content relative to man's behavior with surrounding phenomena, the degrees of cognition will be different among individuals. As teachers work on program development together, they should become learners together and try to ascertain levels of abstraction with respect to the subject-matter content. A simple approach to the organization of the content might be in terms of possible levels of behavior represented as behavior 1, 2, 3, 4, and so on. This would be their conception of the levels of abstraction and may not coincide with those of the children. Since it is difficult to determine levels of abstraction as experienced by someone else, one needs to be "open" to the individual's approach to thinking about abstractions. An important point about this type of program or curriculum development is that teachers are learners and *scholars* who are pursuing high-level meanings without being regimented into a system of regularity as preconceived by institutional design. Teachers as well as children are extending their conception of realities and creating a greater sense of involvement and existence in the structure of knowledge. They are outside of a system which regiments the funneling and delineation of an "encrusted" approach to the continuation of a deadness in knowledge.

In a previous section the question of the use of toys as subject-matter content for the extension of the realities of young children was discussed in considerable detail. The subject matter was used with toys and other articles and objects in connection with related elements and disciplines. The relation of a person's behavior with air and the accompanying development of concepts were treated at length. From this discussion it should be apparent that the use of toys and surrounding phenomena such as air and other elements would provide the structure for extended realities about knowledge and would actually constitute much of the substance for high-level inquiry and the furtherance of one's existence with ideas.

DEVELOPING CONCEPTS ABOUT THE NATURE OF MAN AND HIS BEHAVIOR

The development of concepts of the nature of man is at best a rather speculative undertaking. An exhaustive treatment of it would, take volumes of philosophical thinking. This does not disavow the importance of pursuing knowledge about man's behavior as he relates it to his existence. Man's behavior and its relation to his existence is at the heart of any educational program, since behavior takes into account the knowledge associated with the various disciplines and the structure which opens up the routes of inquiry to it. Yet this type of program is usually at the thin periphery of the regular school curriculum. Also, if a program associated with man and his nature is developed at all, it is usually restricted to the high school and college areas of the school continuum. Rarely is any effort made to provide the impact for young children to regard themselves as behavers, their purposes as people, their concepts of self, and some of the wellsprings of their being.

Since the subject of man's nature and his behavior is so vast and speculative, it is not intended here to approach the major questions associated with it. It is intended rather to indicate some of the ways in which children may begin to think of behavior and how it relates to what one does. Again, it is important that the approach to a knowledge of behavior should probably be made in terms of surrounding phenomena with which children can identify.

Children's concepts of useful behavior may lead to productive confrontations with values. This immediately brings forward some speculation about what useful behavior might be. Concepts of useful behavior vary from person to person, from age groups to age group, and between boys and girls. Children's thinking about useful behavior and their recognition of the variety of the concepts associated with behavior is in itself a most useful initial step in approaching the topic. Also, in the beginning of the approach to the concepts of useful behavior many of the simple ideas about what is useful and what is not can be explored in conversation with children.

Perhaps a major concept relative to the whole question of behavior is that it is ever-present. The point that should be made is that it is important always to behave more than less. This is quite different from the usual idea of behavior. Usually behavior is either regarded as a sort of vague and nondescript entity or as an element that needs to be controlled. As a result the whole question of behavior becomes somewhat absorbed in what have become clichés in the instructional program of the school. The clichés appear in the terms, motivation, readiness, creating interest, taking the child where he is and guiding him as far as he can go, having children work up to their capacity, and providing for individual differences. Behavior as thus conceived somehow does not exist. It is not regarded as extant here, now, and all the time. The structure for developing concepts about behavior should provide the impact which suggests that everyone in a room is behaving at the present time. The teacher would suggest that he is behaving also. All have behaved before this occasion and will do so afterward. The fact becomes apparent that behavior has never stopped—it goes on continuously. In this conception it gradually becomes clear that behavior is a kind of disposition which causes people to attend to an idea, a creation, or getting something done. Another fact is that behavior does not exist separately and by itself, but happens in every topic and subject in a school.

Involved with behavior is the whole system of values which individual behavers hold. The values more or less determine the behaviors employed by each one in his search for greater realization and a higher sense of existence. That views about behavior are frequently not associated with values and the tendency to approach meanings is made apparent by such queries as: Where and when do we teach values? Shouldn't we give some time to the inculcation of moral principles? Why is the period of adolescence such a difficult one to cope with? What do you do to keep children busy when they have finished their work? When is there time in the day to work with values, moral questions, and individual strengths with pupils?

These and other questions indicate a thinking about behavior as something apart—as something that might possibly be avoided. Central to these conceptions of behavior is that it is somehow to be equated with a resistant force. As a result there develops an attitude which ties behavior up with the uncontrolled ones, the resistant ones and often with those in the subculture group.

The whole question of behavior is so overwhelming, in a sense, that it is difficult to treat it in detail in a discourse of this type. Behavior—its directions and affects—is determined by many cultural and value patterns within which people find their being. System after system is developed to control it, to point it, to use it. There is a system of behavior to encompass brotherly compassion, and almost at the same time there is a system that enables behavior to degrade and destroy. There is the technology which harnesses behavior for material production. There are the religious organizations which try to recapture and further one's regard for one's neighbor and a greater sense of humaneness. There are also those organizations which are designed to perpetuate systems with no apparent humane ends. In all of these conditions behavior serves definite purposes of individuals. A vital point, however, to be suggested is that behavior seems to terminate at a certain level. Congealing occurs at different levels for different individuals.

Congealing of behavior at certain points by different individuals occurs in schools. In fact, the school as a system has unwittingly developed built-in stoppage places for behavior. These stoppage places have to some extent already been indicated in the references made to practices associated with motivation, flexibility, measurement, standards, required reading lists, required reading series, and others. The system becomes generally closed at certain levels for most children with a few spurts here and there beyond the confines of the established program.

Man extracts meanings from the phenomena to extend his behav-

ior. As suggested in other sections of this book, he transforms the phenomena into subject-matter content. At the same time he remains attuned to the phenomena for further messages. He therefore expands the content of the disciplines as he encounters the new messages. He is behaving with the content. He becomes more and more involved with it. In this involvement much is happening to him. He becomes increasingly aware of the nature of the disciplines even as he builds the content of the disciplines. As he encounters more meaning he expands the disciplines.

As man relates to the disciplines he is always in confrontation with the phenomena from which the meanings of the subject matter of the disciplines are expanded. The phenomena more or less constitute the centers from which he derives his sense of renewal with the content of the disciplines. Therein he finds relevance and usefulness in his behavior.

As suggested in Chapter 3, man's relationship with meanings is continuously expanded in a condition of openness to messages. Although he retains his identity with the usual roles, he is always beyond himself in retrieving the messages from phenomena with them. To put it bluntly, the nature of man and his behavior in all its ramifications is brought into the school by all those who are to be affected by it.

The thinking about useful behavior is at the heart of the questions relating to man and his predicament. To convey the impact of these questions, those who are involved must bring about the contact points for their encounter with meanings. The experiences of children should be instrumental in producing these contact points. They are actually then a recapitulation of man as he relates interactively with the phenomena and the content of the disciplines. This means that the experiences must not be separately contrived but rather evolved by individuals as they relate to the questions of usefulness in behavior. These questions can then become the focal points for inquiry into the nature of behavior. These may be developed in *centers, laboratories,* location places, or something else. What is important is that they are not "walled in" or in any way separated from the disciplines and the "regular" arrangements. The centers could emphasize invitational aspects through labels that would reflect the active concern of children.

One of these labels might be, "How and what we behave about now." In this connection the matter of when one behaves and how much he behaves is pertinent. Another section of the centers of interest might be involved with behaviors which do not now exist but which might be developed. Questions which could be considered relative to the labels indicated might be: What are the types of topics through which behavior may be indicated? What are the types of knowledges and skills needed for useful behavior? What kinds of arrangements can be provided to bring about more useful behavior?

In connection with the labels to provide the impact to thinking about useful behavior and the questions indicated above, children in talking with their companions might begin thinking of forms of useful behavior in the school. They could consider some ideas of useful behavior they would tell their friends about. In addition, they may begin thinking about the useful behavior involved with their subjects. For example, they might talk about what they think is useful behavior in reading, in their number work, and in the other areas. They can be encouraged to talk with their friends about useful behavior on the way to and from school. They could suggest what they do in the home which they regard as valuable and useful behavior. Then too, they can regard the evidences of useful behavior all around them—what different people do to provide for themselves and their families a really vital existence. As they are thinking about useful behavior in the school, with their friends, or in the community they will begin to expand their life space. They might begin to talk about what people do in other times and places. Much of the substance in their conversation about other times and places will come from what they have viewed on television—and what their parents and other adults and young adults have told them.

In order to promote the conditions which suggest that behavior is extant all the time everywhere and with every task, it might be well to consider the classroom and school as a laboratory for this purpose. One way to promote these conditions could be the designation of a section of the room to *Useful Behavior*. The teacher is the first behaver here as he inquires into ideas of usefulness. Behaviors here might be categorized under captions such as

Our Behavior Now—What, How, When, and How Much.

Behaviors Which Need to Be Developed.

Topics Through Which Behavior Happens.

Knowledges and Skills Needed for Useful Behavior.

Arrangements or Changes Which are Needed to Bring about Useful Behavior.

Children could bring suggestions which would be placed under the labels. These suggestions should, of course, come from the children as they bring their curiosity and imagination into play. Every opportunity should be developed to encourage individual children's offerings to the section on *Useful Behavior*. Their contributions could be presented in the form of clippings, pictures, or drawings.

As suggested above, the structuring of the conditions for the representation of and identification with useful behavior should bring all the powers of children into play. This should be true not only with respect to contributions under the labels but also the development of the categories with which children wish to represent useful behavior. They may want to suggest other labels than those indicated. Furthermore, they may enter all types of labels of their own under those they have indicated as the general ones. As a result, they may bring in labels such as Home, Community, Out-of-School, In Billy's House and others. They may wish to specialize as to different subjects such as Reading, Spelling, Numbers, Social Studies, and Sciences. They may want to have labels which represent behavior all around us such as people's work, people's recreation, and people's devotional tasks, and people's thinking. Then, too, they may just have categories such as Behavior Around Us and Behavior Far from Us. In connection with these various captions children might be encouraged to deal with such topics as the Home and Out-of-School in terms of their behaviors now, behaviors which they need to develop, the knowledges and skills needed, the subjects with which they may acquire the behaviors, and the arrangements which have to be changed to bring about the behaviors. By change of arrangements is meant the provision of those conditions which make accessible the resources which will help extend the realities regarding useful behavior. This means that more books, people, and other communicative media should be encountered for the extension of meanings. Furthermore, centers should evolve where ideas may be developed relative to television programs which should be viewed as most vital resources.

The action and thinking of children relative to the arrangements which they feel are needed for the pursuit of extended meanings not only furnish clues as to how they relate to realities and knowledge but also provide richer content for new points of inquiry. Great teaching will always tend not only to encourage and facilitate these efforts on the part of the pupils, but will find the teacher as a behaver in his own right in these efforts.

As suggested previously, the classroom should assume laboratory conditions to promote inquiry on the part of children with respect to useful behavior. It is to be understood that the efforts to seek meanings regarding useful behavior will involve all the areas of the curriculum. The task then becomes associated with many concepts about useful behavior in subjects and related content. The attitudes and arrangements which are involved here may take a variety of forms, some of which have already been indicated. Another possible arrangement which may not only be representative of children's concepts of useful behavior but may also provide a system of recording the concepts would be the development of a resource file. This file might be called The Story and Practice of Useful Behavior. This file would contain contributions relative to children's immediate behaviors, the needed behaviors, the subjects through which the behaviors might be developed, and others. In fact, the file could be in terms of all the captions, labels, and categories through which the children have decided to represent the topics of Useful Behavior. Sections of the file would probably be labeled as Useful Behavior in Reading, Useful Behavior with Numbers, Useful Behavior with Science, and so on.

In connection with The Story of Useful Behavior and Practice, children as well as teachers would more and more come to a realization that behavior is integrally tied up with all the subject areas and all the activities in which man is engaged. This would range from what people do every day to make a living to the acts they perform that have no appreciable value in the practical sense. In other words, thinkers and "dreamers" about meanings which are not directly related to their work may also exemplify useful behavior. Furthermore, Useful Behavior may take place in the mind without any physical manipulation. Above all, useful behavior should contain the ingredients that will provide identity for the user.

In order that the approach to meanings about useful behavior may not be construed solely as a group project, respective file categories might be developed by individuals. In fact, the study of various categories of useful behavior by different individuals could be their research efforts. A pupil may wish to think, read about, and interview others about useful behavior in promoting good feelings. Another may choose to deal about useful behavior in connection with the study of birds. Still another may decide to show behavior with number relationships. These individuals and others will further their inquiry about these topics wherever and whenever the occasion permits. They may wish to report their studies to the other children so that their concepts of usefulness may find new connections and, perhaps, suggest new directions of inquiry. The reports should also provide the occasion for setting up communicative situations where the thinking of those engaged on research or other items may bring that thinking to bear on each other's sense of extended realities. Frequently, the one who is close to a certain meaning may become blinded to other possibilities. Those possibilities might be brought into awareness by various opportunities for confrontation with other children.

Another form of study of useful behavior may be the analysis of the types of representations which children made of the various categories of useful behavior over a period of time. For example, as certain individuals had indicated the behavior they were pursuing presently, they probably considered the behaviors which were needed, then what skills and knowledges were needed, and so on. After a period of following through with the various labels they might take a new sheet and try to indicate the behaviors without reference to the original recording. After this they would look at the original recording, compare it with the later one, and note the changes that had taken place in what they regarded as useful behavior. As children examine and discuss the differences between the two records of behavior, they gain concepts about change, about new values, about learning, and possibly about how one begins to grow up. They note especially about how their concepts of usefulness had changed and how they as people had taken on new meanings about reality and existence. Children begin to comprehend something about people and how they behave. As they think about it, they talk about usefulness now and how they used to talk about it.

As has been indicated previously, the development of extended realities about man and his behavior encompasses an overwhelming number of experiences and would take volumes to attempt an explanation. Yet the overwhelming nature of this subject does not lessen its importance as substance for the learning experiences of children. A number of illustrations and detailed suggestions about subject-matter treatment of man and his behavior have been indicated through the medium of the topic, Useful Behavior. The treatment is by no means exhaustive. Enough has been dealt with in connection with this topic, however, to suggest some direction in instruction and program development in the area of behavior with young children. It is difficult to say what the outcomes should be relative to concept development. To try to detail some would be restrictive. It is hoped that the suggestions indicated are only beginnings and that skilled teachers will help develop those settings which will extend the realities of young children regarding man and his behavior beyond what anybody had imagined. One must hasten to suggest that children's thinking on this great topic beyond what teachers anticipated should occasion no surprise to the teachers. Great teaching was always thus.

chapter 5

Some Thoughts About the Nature of Science and Quantitative Meanings

One of the features of the open system of inquiry is that all knowledge should be in the purview of everyone regardless of his age level and experiential background. In the closed system, knowledge is divided into parts ranging from the easier-portions to the more difficult. A young child has the easier parts allotted to him. The portions are graduated in difficulty for the child as he goes on through the continuum. Furthermore, there is usually a sharp division line between the parts, the assumption being that each part gives the needed background for the succeeding part, that learning proceeds from the simple to the complex as thought out by the teacher, the curriculum worker, or someone else. Also, the dose of learning becomes bigger as the child grows older. In the closed system it would then follow that major questions relating to the sciences and mathematics would not be dealt with by young children, except perhaps in a very miniscule way.

EXTENDED MEANINGS THROUGH A DETERMINATION OF THE NATURE OF PHYSICAL QUALITIES

In the open system of inquiry, topics such as *The Nature of Physical Qualities* would certainly be brought within the orbit of the child's as well as a teacher's experiencing regardless of the age levels. It is not meant here to make everyone a physicist. Rather, what is intended is to approach the structure of knowledge in topics of the type suggested so that the principle of inquiry into these topics will provide an awareness to the various domains of knowledge. An awareness to the structure and its content will bring into focus the messages of the topic. The gradual accretion of messages will in turn expand the capacity of the mind for the transformation of experience.

Physical qualities are a fact in all the surrounding phenomena in the environment. To bring them into focus for human encounter necessitates perhaps some deviation from the "regularized" forms of inquiry. It would seem then that every individual in this encounter must be a first behaver in developing a sense of awareness to the messages of the various media associated with physical qualities. The teacher as a first behaver on his own part would begin to reflect on some central factors regarding the topic. As a first behaver he confronts children whose minds also have encountered the impact of physical qualities. They perhaps would think first of all of the body as being associated with the physical. Inquiry about the body may reveal functioning organs, shape, form, a mechanism of bones, a covering of muscles intertwined with tissues, a network of nerves, a brain, and so on. Many ideas about the nature of the body would be derived—many of them biological, others chemical, and still others neurological. The inquiry could bring all knowledge about the nature of the body into the child's domain of experiences. There would develop concepts of how the body transforms food, air, water, and other elements into a functioning whole; concepts about procreation, about coordination, and about locomotion. The whole question of health would come into focus. The importance of the physical qualities of the body would certainly be portrayed by all the media directed to it—not the least of these being television.

In connection with the development of conditions whereby many media may be encountered, it is important for a classroom not to limit meanings. Rather, the classroom may be just the "front or back door" which opens the mind to seek for the greater meanings outside of it. As the teacher actually is the first behaver in involving himself with extended observations of phenomena, so will the children become first behavers in extending the area for derivation of meanings. It is suggested most emphatically that the discourse which follows with the illustrations and patterns may be rounded out with many alternatives that may extend the bases for the extraction of messages and meanings.

Physical qualities are encountered in inquiry about materials. Inquiry here may lead to some concepts about weight, solids, liquids, connections, and extended relationships about topics of this type. Direction toward this type of inquiry might develop with questions such as the following: As you were handling toys and other objects, you perhaps noted that they had shape and form. No doubt you also noted that much color was associated with the toys. What other ideas did you get about the toys and objects as you played with them? All types of responses will be evoked as children think about what they do with the toys. For example, a pupil might observe that some of the toys are heavy and some light. Another might think of some toys being made of one, two, or three pieces of wood or metal while others have dozens of parts. Some toys would be easier to take apart and put together than others. Some toys might break more easily than others. (This fact in itself could be the starting point of a whole cluster of observations about breakable and nonbreakable materials. The question which might arise is whether breakable materials are of lighter weight than the more durable ones.)

As children become involved with the nature of materials, other items might be introduced into this setting for inquiry. Thought about the quality of substance may be extended by bringing many types of boxes or containers, some holding various items and other empty; heavy or solid boxes and very light ones. Some of the boxes would contain blocks of wood, some would have only one heavy or light article, others would contain various weights of liquids. Still others would contain connected articles, while others would enclose separate items.

It will indeed be interesting to observe children to see how they relate their thinking to the handling of the boxes. Some children may decide to classify the boxes in terms of weight, others to put together all those boxes that contain about the same things. Some children may attempt to guess what is in the boxes by shaking them. Others will try to decide whether the pieces in the boxes are separate or connected. Some children will try to guess which of the boxes contain metal and which contain wooden pieces. Any number of reactions and responses of children will come forth as they are working with the boxes. As a more or less detached member of the group and as a learner, the teacher will take note of the responses of the children in order to ascertain how they relate to the acquisition of meanings—that is, how different individuals make inferences from examining the boxes, and so on. The teacher will also take note as to how different individuals examine the boxes and their reasons for doing so. The teacher might try to determine how individuals seek to gain meaning about the boxes and contents. The teacher would make some inquiry about the boxes too. He could be observant relative to the way individuals go about establishing meanings about solids and liquids, about lightweight and heavyweight materials. Observations could be made as to how children make use of language in their questioning. It is important to be aware of a child's expression of a need even if he does not have the ability to fulfill it. The awareness of the need on the part of the child and the sensitivity of the teacher to the child's expression will serve to give some direction to future confrontation for learning.

The awareness of the teacher should not be limited to those children who indicate a need for further information. The teacher should help develop the conditions where all children may have a free flow of expression relative to their thinking. The bases of their inferences

should be noted, for many of these indicate some intuitive understandings of relationships. The ideas of children and the manner in which
they arrived at them should reveal many clues to the teacher for the
extension of the learning environment.

   Physical qualities give meaning to behavior. Physical qualities are
a fact in the environment. The individual's employment of his environment brings him into continual contact with physical phenomena. He
behaves with them and at the same time observes their behavior. For
example, one behaves with cold, heat, water, air, trees, sun, shade, and
with many other phenomena. As individuals relate to cold, heat, and so
on the behavior is more or less obvious and automatic and is usually not
pointed up as having meanings. Actually the behavior is fraught with
meanings which may be brought into focus with questions such as: In
what different ways does heat behave? What happens when heat and
cold come together? How are seasons related to heat and cold? These
and other questions will bring many meanings into the setting for learning relative to physical quality. For example, clothes become a factor,
as do seasons, shade, trees, water, and other related elements. Other
questions which may result are: Why is water cooler than the surrounding air? Why is it cooler in the shade than in the sun? The whole
question of the quality of the sun may come into consideration.

   In relation to the above questions, many meanings will be developed in which scientific principles are involved. Some of these will
relate to the sun and its power. Others will relate to the nature of heat,
cold, and the behavior of air. Terms such as rays, heat conduction,
density, and penetration will take on various meanings for individuals.

   As children inquire into the numerous questions that relate to
phenomena, their curiosity will extend to other observations. As children view themselves in relation to the behavior of physical qualities
they come to look at their own behavior in a similar light. They thus put
themselves into question. They are considering what happens to them
as well as to the physical things which they encounter. Teachers do the
same as they relate to physical phenomena. Children in their questions
and inquiry become involved with many items or objects in their approach to meanings. Some of these are solid objects such as sticks,
stones, marbles, balls, and others. Some of these objects are smooth and
others are not. For example, a marble has a smooth rounded surface, as
does a ball. They may compare the behavior of smooth rounded objects
with smooth surfaces—a marble, when it is rolled on a smooth surface,
behaves quite differently than when it is rolled on a rough surface. This
fact takes on some meaning to children who play marbles. Some children may venture an explanation of the behavior of marbles on different
surfaces. They may contrive the arrangements for an experiment such

as putting different things in the marble's path—sand, for example—so as to slow its momentum. Children would have different explanations to give meaning to their observations. Some would say that the sand slows down the marble. Others would say that it acts somewhat like a brake on a car. The discussion about this will move the thinking into other relationships, even to the type of braking used to stop a jet after it lands. The thinking would become involved with different methods used in slowing things down. Different behaviors would be explored.

As children think about the behavior of rolling objects they would consult books, television, and other media. Their explanations would be extended, perhaps into the behavior of a baseball, tennis ball, and football. Also, they would relate to the behavior of people with a ball. They would suggest that a ball can be thrown, batted, kicked, bounced, shoved, or maneuvered. Furthermore, they would suggest the behaviors of spectators in ballgames.

The above illustrations and discussion does not, of course, exhaust the approach to meanings about the behavior of physical phenomena. It should be clear, however, that the pupils are in the position of the first behavers with meanings and regarded as such by the teachers. They are relating themselves to knowledge in terms of their perceptions. They are entering into the subject matter in the way they relate to meanings. They are extracting ideas that will tend to clarify their behaviors to themselves. The teachers become learners with the pupils. They should become cognizant as to how children relate to knowledge and how they select out the meanings that provide areas for further quests. The teachers, viewing each child as a first behaver, will become conversant with the different ways in which he derives meanings and thus effect a confrontation with him. The teachers, confronting children in the development of meanings and content, will thereby not only help produce each individual child but will further produce themselves relative to the differences. They will be learners and teachers together.

It was suggested that in the open system each individual extends his domain of inquiry. It is clear from the above discourse that this should be happening. As teachers and children locate key questions, each extends his domain of inquiry. Never are the routes to knowledge diminished. They are constantly enlarged and multiplied. More and more contact points for meanings emerge as knowledge inquired into extends into expanded relationships. Curiosity is enlarged, new connections to old meanings are discovered, and more and more resources and men of great seminal thought are brought into the setting for teaching and learning. Thus the domains of inquiry become expanded, and although anchor points to meaning are present, attempts at confinement or final completion are guarded against.

The additional resources and the connections with surrounding phenomena come about spontaneously as teachers and children tend to inquire and probe into ideas. There is no "dragging in" of resources and phenomena, no tendency to "clutter up" with these before the connection points are ascertained. Rather the incursion of the surrounding phenomena and resources are by invitation. The invitation is a two-way street—the individuals "invite in" the resources as they approach extended meanings in their inquiry, and in turn find an inviting entrance to the resources as a greater fulfillment of their existence with knowledge. As new phenomena give meaning to the behavior of individuals they become a part of the subject-matter content.

DEVELOPING EXTENDED REALITIES ABOUT QUANTITATIVE MEANINGS

Educators often recommend that there should be a minimum of formal arithmetic in the early grades of school. By formal here is meant the inculcation of number facts which are to be developed mostly for future use. For example, in this formal approach, counting and learning of number names would come first, followed by addition facts, then subtraction and so on. Almost in the same breath, it is usually suggested that number work should involve many applications of a practical nature. Also, it is suggested that there should be many number manipulative activities. In other words, instead of grappling with the abstract concept of six, the child should look at six *things* and handle them. It is frequently suggested that the approach to number meanings with children should be very informal.

Generally speaking, the informal approach to meaningful development should be used not only with number but with all other subject-matter content. By informal we do not mean the avoidance of abstract number relationships. Too often the concept of formal is associated with the abstract. By the same token, formal seems to be equated with the difficult. This type of generalization is open to serious question. Informal procedures in the development of meanings may be very closely tied up with abstract number relationships.

A simple structuring of conditions for number meaning may exist where 16 buttons and 7 beans are found on different sections of a table. Children might be asked to try to ascertain the differences in the two items. One difference, of course, would be that one could not use buttons the same way as beans. Someone may suggest this. If the two sets of items cannot be used in the same way, they cannot be mixed up. As children study the beans and buttons separately one might suggest the question of How Many. Another difference, then, will in time become evident—that there are more buttons than beans on the table. The word *equal* may be introduced in connection with the word *difference.* The two items then are not equal. Efforts may be made to find out how many more buttons there are than beans. Granted that some children have learned to count, counting would be one way of discovering how many more buttons there are than beans. But there are other ways of finding out differences in quantities. One would be to line the buttons and beans up one by one—one button with one bean—until it was clear that there were more buttons. Children in this connection may become acquainted with words and terms such as more, fewer, unequal, matching one to one, and others. At this time children might also become conscious about groupings of items. Some could then observe how many equal groups of buttons they could make out of 16 buttons and, similarly, how many they could make out of the beans. Then they could also match groups of buttons with groups of beans and ascertain the differences in quantities through counting beyond the equal groups. The problem of making the two items equal in quantity is much more complicated than one at first suspects. A question might be related to the additional number needed in one item to make it equal with the other item. How could this be determined? What would one count, and what would the unknown number be called?

As these questions are being considered by the children the matter of number symbols might be brought in. The unknown number might be called $a, x,$ or most anything until the true quantity is found, in which case it might be designated as 9. One item, no doubt, would have to be stated as $9x$ while another would have to be $9y$, or some such designation. As children become conscious of the use of symbols, a somewhat different structuring might be brought into the conditions for learning. They might be asked to show in as many different ways as they can what nine means. In their responses, they might think of 9 things, or they might think of 3 and 6 or 3 and 3 and 3. Then, too, some children may bring in the question of quantities and equals, and suggest that 3 and 2 and 4 is the same as 3 and 5 and 1. Some children will, of course, indicate other combinations of equations.

In the process of working with equations the conditions should include arrangements as to objects For example, children could try to supply the X in the following: $X + 10$ checkers $+ 5$ checkers $+ X = 25$ checkers. For other purposes the equation could read $X + 10$ checkers $+ 10$ checkers $= 5$ checkers $+ 15$ checkers $+ X$. Any number of equations may be represented in connection with different objects. From this one could gradually go into symbolic representations without reference to objects. The same process used in connection with whole numbers can also be used in representing concepts about fractions. A useful form of structuring to develop concepts about fractions is to represent some object associated with children which can be shown by parts. All the parts together would represent the whole object. The object shown in either three, four, or five parts would have the parts designated by the symbols 3, 4, and 5. However, in thinking of the object as a whole we have to designate it as 1. But in representing it in parts they have to be designated as a quarter, as a half, or as a third. These symbols are made clear in the confrontation which takes place among the children and teacher. The equation relative to fractions, then, can be stated as one-quarter   one-quarter   one-half   one. In symbolic terms this, of course, would be represented as

$$\tfrac{1}{4} + \tfrac{1}{4} + \tfrac{1}{2} = 1.$$

To take this a step further to develop speculative thinking relative to equations we could at first designate this representation of parts by

$$X + \tfrac{1}{4} + \tfrac{1}{2} = 1.$$

Find the value of X. Then, the whole could be represented as

$$X + \tfrac{1}{2} = \tfrac{1}{2} + X.$$

X, of course, in this case, is always the unknown. The child's intuitive thinking should in most cases determine the value of X.

The suggestions which have been made are not exhaustive of the possibilities for the development of abstract number relationships. In a classroom there should be all kinds of number relationships in a learning environment. Children will want to spend so much time that it will be difficult to attract them to other important activities. Children will indeed, respond to activities and experiences associated with abstract number relationships. Here they will respond to the point of extending their conception of realities.

Another form of structuring which may be developed in connection with number relationships is that of number decades. This, too, is associated with equations but in a rather concrete manner. For example, since $3 + 6 = 9$,

$$3 + 16 = (10 \text{ more than } 9) \quad \text{or } 19.$$

Three   26 would then be two 10's more than 9 or 29. Three $+ 36$ then could be $9 + 10 + 10 + 10$, thus indicating 3 10's and 9. This would certainly suggest a rather interesting exercise with the decade of tens on the basis of nine which could be used with any other number—in a similar manner. This type of exercise may also be used as a form of initial approach to the understanding of the decimal system.

It was hinted at in a previous section that the use of practical applications to establish number meanings is often considered as the antithesis of abstraction. This is not necessarily true. In approaching the development of the concept of multiplication, for example, the question of how many hamburgers would be needed for a picnic for the members of a classroom might produce the type of confrontation needed for the understanding of the process of multiplication. The thinking of course should not be delineated for the children. Rather, the conditions should be provided whereby the children study several arithmetic processes together—that is, multiplication as repeated addition of equals and division as a process of subtraction of equals. The whole question of the advantages of one process over another would be fully examined. More important, the decimal system as it works in both the multiplication and division process would be intensively explored. The fact that in arithmetic the changes in quantity arrived at through the processes really do not alter anything can be widely experienced through various settings for insight into number relationships. The principle of substitution of one or two quantities for another should sooner or later become clear to at least some children.

For the purpose of gaining insight into mathematical meanings on the abstract level the classroom should be provided with mathematical laboratory situations. Arrangements which will enable children to manipulate numbers to determine relationships have already been indicated as being helpful in gaining insights as to grouping of numbers and the handling of simple equations. In the laboratory arrangements, place value boxes should be accessible to children so that they can become conversant with the decimal system. There should be centers or "corners" where number relations may be seen in their different decades. All types of objects—wooden rods of different sizes, and other items—should be available in laboratory cabinets to help children learn about equations, the different number processes, and the principle of number substitution. There should be pocket charts on which children can manipulate the processes of addition, subtraction, multiplication, and division both with whole numbers and with fractions. The most important feature of a mathmetics laboratory, however, is where children will have the opportunity for inventiveness in their efforts to gain meanings about number relationships. They should be encouraged to develop ways in which they will facilitate their methods of inquiry into the processes of multiplication and division, for example.

In developing the conditions for inventiveness on the part of children in their approach to abstract number it might be suggested that they try to ascertain what makes sense, for example, in the various processes. If a child said that 3 x 3 = 6 one might ask if he looked at his symbol between the 3's. If the symbol was a *plus* sign he would be correct. Since it is, however, a *times* sign he needs to think of three 3's. If, however, multiplication is still too difficult for him to comprehend, he might decide how he still can use the plus or addition in trying to determine the value of three 3's. He could put the threes in an array of three pairs of three dots and then determine the value of three 3's. If he arrived at 9 by the times route he might then think of how many 3's there are in 9, which he could grasp through addition or subtraction of equals. In connection with this, he should be urged to give attention to the results in the two processes employed—addition and subtraction as used for division. In the subtraction of equals, for example, he would need to count each equal he took out until there was no number left. In addition, he would need to count the equals he added until he arrived at the number he added up to.

Children should be encouraged to develop ways which might make it easier for them to grasp concepts of more than one process at the same time. The following is just a suggestion as to one of the ways in which concepts relative to multiplication and division may be developed. As noted in Fig. 5-1, the child will be multiplying the figures in

		7	21			7
		6	18			6
		5	15			5
		4	12			4
		3	9			3
		2	6			2
3	X	1	3	÷	3	1
		28	84	÷	3	28

Fig. 5-1. Concept development in multiplication and division.

the first column by 3 and then dividing the results in the second column by 3. By dividing the numbers in the second column by 3, the results in the fourth column will indicate the same numbers as those in the first column. The operation here is one of doing and undoing. Through the inverse operation with the second column by means of division, the child should experience some concepts of number relationships as between multiplication and division. An added feature for some children could be a set of cards indicating multiplication as repeated addition and a set which could suggest division as subtraction of equals. If, for example, a child was in doubt about 3 X 4 being equal to 12, he would look for the card containing the multiplicand of 4 with four 3's on it. In division he would find the dividend 12 card and observe on it the subtraction of four 3's. Variations to the use of these patterns suggested in Fig. 5-1 could be the counting by 3's until the number indicated by the multiplier has been reached. For division a mark for the number of 3's counted out of the dividend would be put down until zero was reached. Rather than making a chart as indicated in Fig. 5-1 each child could have accessible to him a pocket chart and number cards with which he could improvise ever so many approaches to concepts about interrelationships of number processes. The pocket charts could also be used in representing and manipulating the principle of equals in equations and number substitutions.

The various approaches to number meanings and abstractions are not intended to disavow the importance of number facts as usually conceived. It is important that they should be learned. The purpose, however, is to indicate that number facts need to be developed in their total relationships in order to establish abstract meanings about them. Then they truly become not only separate facts but principles of structure for mathematical knowledge. While children are working with number relationships and abstractions they and the teachers are building a high-level structure for more intensive inquiry into extended realities about number. In other words, the program substance for responsive occupation with mathematical ideas is being continually broadened and extended.

DEVELOPING EXTENDED REALITIES WITH SCIENCE EXPERIENCES

A great deal of treatment has already been given in the section on the use of toys to extend meanings about science and related phenomena. Accordingly, it will be dealt with briefly here. It is important to isolate certain elements relative to science so that concrete concepts may be developed to the point of extending the curiosity of the child in this subject. It is hoped that this will enable him to feel a sense of compulsion to inquire even more intensively into the surrounding phenomena for scientific meanings. Although it is always important to encourage the child to seek knowledge in terms of relationships, there is a danger that the whole structure of meanings will become so complicated that he will find it difficult to pick salient features to help him in his pursuit of scientific ideas. It always reinforces a child's sense of inquiry to be able to take hold of a few concepts as starting and generating points for further meanings. He needs some anchors around which he can build knowledge and locate himself with it. Anchor points, however, should constitute the "stations" of freedom toward intriguing areas of inquiry.

In a previous section of this chapter much was suggested as to ways in which children might be helped to develop concepts about the subject, air. It was suggested, for example, that air is substance, occupies space, and is involved with heat and cold, and so on. The ideas might be extended into the various ways in which one's behavior is affected by air. Again, this would relate to heat and cold. Furthermore, new relationships might be established in terms of one's behavior and ingenuity in extending the behavior in the production of comfort. For example, a person behaves in an adaptive manner relative to the clothes he produces and uses and the shelter he has designed. In this connection, the meaning of the various seasons would be brought into a clear sense of cognition. The principles of air conditioning and insulation could here become a part of one's identification with comfort. Children could learn something about the use of fans and what is happening to hot air, for example, in the air-conditioning process. Questions would arise as to whether air is cooled or changed. Questions, also, would arise relative to where the *hot air* goes and where the *cool air comes* from when the air is warm all around us. The task of the teacher becomes tremendously important in that he needs to develop conditions which contain not only the ingredients for messages related to scientific meanings but which bring about a sense of inventiveness with these meanings on the part of the children. The conditions have to enable a child to locate himself with scientific ideas so that he will make a real transfer to the point of internalization of the ideas with his existence. He will, in effect, advance into a real conversation with the ideas.

As the questions are being pursued relative to man's behavior with air, a related topic such as the nature of water could be brought into the setting for scientific inquiry. Many additional questions will emerge here. Why do they say "Keep your head above water"? Is drowning related to air? Isn't there a certain amount of water in the air at all times? Is there more at some times than others? At this point the concept of humidity may be established as well as other related aspects. If air contains water, is it also true that water contains air? If so, why can you not submerge and live? As these questions are being developed, other penetrations will be made into the subject of man's behavior with water. These would revolve around questions of our need for water to sustain life, the use of water to facilitate vegetation, and the structure of water relative to buoyancy, power, and seeking its own level. Other questions would involve the use of water in plants, vegetables, fruit, and living bodies. It would be found, for example, that vegetables such as potatoes and turnips are largely made up of water and that fruit such as apples and peaches are also mostly water. Somehow, the conditions should provide for reflective observations so that many messages may be encountered and confronted for high-level meanings. Through observations rather than through answers children will become located with facts and generalizations which in turn will open up new and extended location places for extracting meanings.

In developing the setting for the study of surrounding phenomena such as water, air, and other elements, it is always important to provide the impetus for observation. Initially this should be associated with simple activities. For example, to gain meanings about the topic of water children should be encouraged to observe what it does. How is it different from land? How do liquids behave as compared to solids? Why does water run? Are there conditions where water becomes solid? Why do clouds drop water? How does the water get into the clouds? These and other questions will arise as children observe the behavior of water and think and talk about it. From simple observations certain generalizations are derived, and on these more extended and perhaps more abstract observations will be developed by some children. Some pupils will begin to see the relationship of water and air to weather. The phenomena associated with the formation of weather elements such as rain, snow, and ice will be pursued. This in turn will produce concepts in connection with man's behavior about weather. Concepts regarding shelter, apparel, heating, drying, freezing, and other topics will come within the range of experiences of young children.

One of the most vital relationships of man to water is in recreation and conservation. Water provides opportunities for swimming, water skiing, boating, and fishing. Water is also used by many animals. The whole movement about the conservation of natural resources relates largely to water and its uses by people and animals.

Many scientific and social questions are associated with water and its relation to living things and their existence. The scientific is involved with the larger problem of balance in nature. The problem here also becomes connected to the question of health and well-being of individuals and groups of people. In the zeal to approach scientic questions relative to these problems, individuals by their own ineptitude may bring about conditions that may lead to a deterioration of our living space. A case we have already mentioned is that of the water pollution that has developed over the years as a result of scientific and economic activities in the direction of industrial growth. Whereas industrial development has been instrumental in raising the level of living in many respects, it has at the same time unwittingly brought about conditions which are already interfering with plant and animal life, including human existence.

Recreation, conservation, and the extension of human life becomes involved with the whole question of human values. It cannot be too strongly emphasized that some of the major points of inquiry among individuals should be related to the values and the questions that arise in this pursuit, such as the following: When the cause of water pollution is ascertained, what does it tell us about what some individuals might value as important? When one looks at the whole matter of progress, what are some of the concerns that occur to us? Is the matter of *care* related to progress? What are some of the values that individuals entertain when they talk about various types of progress or good things for people? What are some of the questions one needs to consider when studying the problem of water pollution? As we relate ourselves to this problem, what might be some of the immediate points of inquiry we would undertake?

The above questions are associated with values as regards water pollution. As one relates himself to these values, however, it would soon become apparent that they extend beyond this topic. Associated with water pollution would be questions of recreation, especially as they pertain to impoverished conditions. Children and teachers could become involved with impoverishment as it exists with different people and in different places. While some people live in life extension conditions, others must reside in a state of deprivation. Why are some denied what others have? Are some actually denied what others have, or have the means of acquisition been constricted for them? What elements of concern may make us lucid about how deprivation areas may be eliminated by those who have been victims of these areas?

In the inquiry which should develop relative to these questions, it is important that the approach should be in terms of what *is* rather than what *should* be. Central to this approach is that teachers and children need to discover to what degree they are part of the problem they are trying to solve. Perhaps even more important is an initial recognition and admission that each individual is part of the problem he is trying to inquire about. In a very real sense the area of confrontation is in our immediate presence.

A major reason for the development of the type of impact toward inquiry indicated above is to go beyond a cognition level of approaching the location places of meaning. Simple conceptualizing is not enough. The ingredients which establish a real feeling must be present if a deep sense of concern about an idea is to be engendered. For example, although newspapers and other media depict the conditions of deprivation which are present in a ghetto, a real encounter with what these conditions do to individuals must be experienced *before* the messages which are there are internalized for concern and response. In order to acquire real meaning about ghettos, teachers and children must have a face-to-face confrontation with the types of deprivation prevalent in them. It is just not enough to read about it and merely deplore such conditions generally.

Another area of science which may be approached with young children is that of sound. This is an area rich in opportunities for making observations. As children begin to think of sound, they will begin to observe the varieties of it associated with such terms as yelling, screeching, screaming, high voices, low voices, high tones, low tones, and many others. Certainly the many opportunities for experiences with music should be productive in developing concepts about sound. Obviously, sound media of all types are ever-present in the child's locale. The structuring for the approach to meanings about sound should provide forms of simple experimentation. Children should have the opportunity to contrive the arrangements for producing simple sounds. Again, it is important for teachers to provide the impact for making observations about the behavior of sound. For example, the sound of the wind can be observed as it whistles through narrow openings. Another experience would be to blow over a bottle or small glass and observe the different sounds they can be made. The children can try stringing a thin wire from one classroom to another and ask the children of the other classroom to listen while they pluck the wire with their fingers. The experience with different sounds can be had by tapping tumblers filled with water to different levels.

As children observe how various sounds are produced through the simple experiences indicated, they will tend to extend their inquiry to more complex aspects. They will be ready to generalize about the relationship of air and sound. With these generalizations gathered, children will begin to note how sound is produced by different musical instruments. They may attempt to classify the instruments as those that produce sound by air pressure and those that produce sound through the principle of vibration. Both types, of course, are related to air. In connection with their observations the children could inquire further into the whole subject of sound by making marimbas, horns, and other instruments. All these experiences would certainly tend to expand the realities of children and establish a sense of greater existence with new meanings.

The development of the settings which will stimulate observation relative to surrounding phenomena requires great imagination to detect the ways in which different children associate themselves with elements of simple strangeness. Therefore, one has to speculate as to what impactful situations are to be placed into the learning environment to produce responsive inquiry.

It may be important for children to begin approaching meanings about sound by observing varieties of sound and how they are produced. It is, perhaps, even more important to make observations about how sounds are heard. In this connection, children might be encouraged to observe the vocabulary which relates to the nature of sound. Thus they may begin to grasp the ideas in the words *hear, audible, audition, vibrant, aural, reception,* and others. In this connection, concepts relative to the physical process of receiving sound may be developed. Children might observe the outer structure of the ear and try to arrive at some generalizations as to how this structure relates to the sensation of sound. Some children may possibly inquire further into the structure of the ear by securing plastic models of it. More ingenious children may discover different types of devices used in communication to detect sound. All individuals will gain concepts about such sound media as television and recording. They will hear as much or more than they see.

McLuhan, in several publications, has suggested that ours has become a print culture. Individuals receive their messages by the use of sight. Messages received through a single sense could be restrictive in retrieval of meaning. People are bombarded at all times through the media of television with messages for the ear. Still the major medium for the acquisition of meaning is the printed page. The approach to meanings, therefore, continues in the linear medium provided by the print culture. Thus there exist elements of distortion about what the real messages are. It appears imperative that due attention be given to all the media so as to establish the conditions of attunement to the messages which are resident in these media. The whole sensorium of the human body becomes the reception center rather than just the eye. Humans need tends to become attuned to a whole complex of messages. Perhaps the confrontation with meanings must be with a mosaic rather than with a linear condition.

The above discussion would suggest that individuals experience all types of sounds, linear and complex, and develop a sensitivity to the human expressions that these represent. Many senses have to be brought into play. One has to sense sounds of love, of deep concern, of anxiety, of anger, of rage, and frustration. One needs to become conversant with the meanings conveyed through a form of tribalism. An example of this might be the expression of marchers for causes such as those involved in the singing of "We Shall Overcome." Individuals need to confront with the deep-seated anxieties, loves, and hopes which are exemplified by this type of singing expression. While love and deep-seated anxieties and hopes may comprise the messages of one type of sound, frustration, hates, and deep-seated antagonisms may be the messages of another type.

Although the emphasis here has been in connection with sound, the meanings or messages become much more extensive and far-reaching than sound if all senses are involved. For example, although angry sounds may be the signal for riots if all the senses are attuned to this condition, most if not all the consequences that ensue are envisioned before they occur.

As individuals and groups become conversant with many messages, they may grow inventive in using the messages in a real confrontation through dialogue. This could be a condition wherein individuals would be productive of one another. Experiencing of this type with sound and its relationship with human expression and motivation is indeed a very significant element in promoting a real sense of human existence with children and young people.

In the discussion of the previous pages, most of the emphasis is focused on direct experiencing and experimentation. It is not intended, however, to underestimate the importance of making accessible books, models, materials, and pictures of all kinds which suggest many ideas about topics like air, water, sound, and related phenomena. In fact, much of the stimulus to further inquiry will be provided by these resources. Not only should there be an abundant supply of books and other materials but more should be developed by children as they bring their imagination into play relative to the science topics. Children should be encouraged at every step to develop their ideas in writing, in pictures, in selected clippings and pictures from magazines, and in various forms of creative representation. In these efforts the thinking and imagination of children will be extended. Furthermore, in children's representations of concepts relative to such topics as have been indicated, many clues as to how they relate to knowledge and extended realities should be ascertained.

It is impossible in limited space to give an exhaustive treatment of the infinite number of possibilities involved in the development of extended realities with children in the areas of science. Enough has been discussed, however, to suggest multiple directions in the pursuit of meanings on topics in which scientific aspects are involved. There are many others, such as the whole group of topics related to machines, ideas about new materials for new uses, the meanings which may be derived from an intensive study of the earth in its immediate relationship to one's behavior, some of the simple principles of body development, and many other areas. Much can be learned with children, for example, in digging shallow holes in different types of soil to show texture—gravel or solid soil particles, evidence of presence or lack of moisture, and the make-up of extraneous matter. Also, in this connection the life-giving strength and properties of soil may be tested by detecting the nourishment visible in vegetation.

Other topics which may be pursued are those which deal with life which exists in water. Children who have access to the sea or lakes might raise such questions as the following. Since air is needed for life, how can fish live in the water? Do shellfish need air to live and grow? If so, how do these living things breathe? How are the bodies of these living things different from ours? These and other questions would trigger a whole new set of relationships in the thinking of children. The thinking would be disclosing the interrelationships between water and air. The connections of air and water would also be extended to the soil in these questions: Are there living things in soil? If so, is there air in soil? Do roots of plants as well as leaves need air? The relationships of water and air could also be extended to the human body. Questions and concepts relating to the use of air in parts of the body other than the lungs would no doubt emerge. Facts and concepts would develop relative to breathing as a process applicable not only to humans but to plants and all living things including those in the water. There is no end to the development of extended realities with young children through the resources which have been discussed in detail. This is true not only about children but also about teachers. All are behavers and learners together. All will come to inquire intensively into the surrounding phenomena. This will become the measure of existence which extends beyond the regularized expectancies regarding knowledge.

SELECTED READINGS

Ashton-Warner, Sylvia. *Teacher.* New York: Bantam Books, 1963.

Berman, Louise M. (ed.). *The Humanist and the Curriculum.* Washington, D.C.: Association for Supervision and Curriculum Development, NEA, 1967.

Boyer, William, and Paul Walsh. "Are Children Born Unequal?" *Saturday Review,* October 19, 1968.

Brauner, Charles J., and Hobert W. Burns. *Problems in Education and Philosophy.* Englewood Cliffs, N.J.: Prentice-Hall, 1965. Chapters 4–5.

Bruner, Jerome S. *The Process of Education.* Cambridge: Harvard U. P., 1961.

Elam, Stanley (ed.). *Education and the Structure of Knowledge.* Chicago: Rand-McNally, 1964.

Emerson, Ralph Waldo. "Education" in Reginald L. Cook (ed.), *Ralph Waldo Emerson: Selected Prose and Poetry.* New York: Holt, 1950.

Froebel, Friedrich. *Pedagogics of the Kindergarten.* New York: Appleton, 1895.

———. The Education of Man. New York: Appleton, 1901.

Jackson, Philip W. *Life in Classrooms.* New York: Holt, 1968.

Kessen, William. *The Child.* New York: Wiley, 1965, pp. 274–299.

Leeper, Robert R. (ed.). *Humanizing Education: The Person in the Process.*

Washington, D.C.: Association for Supervision and Curriculum Development, NEA, 1967, pp. 1-19, 42-64, 73-89.

———. (ed.). *Educational Leadership.* Vol. 26, No. 7 (April 1969), pp. 646-661, 693-703.

Miel, Alice, (ed.). *Creativity in Teaching.* Belmont, Calif.: Wadsworth, 1961, pp. 10-77, 107-176.

Montessori. *The Montessori Method.* New York: Stokes, 1912.

Piaget, Jean. *Play, Dreams, and Imitation in Childhood.* New York: Norton, 1962.

Starkey, Margaret M. (ed.). *The Education of Modern Man.* New York: Pitman, 1966.

Suchman, Richard. *The Elementary School Training Program in Scientific Inquiry.* Urbana, Ill.: Research Board, University of Illinois, 1962.

Thelen, Herbert A. *Education and the Human Quest.* New York: Harper, 1960.

chapter 6

On Relating to the Arts, Social Studies, and Other Matters

Every child more or less continuously tries to locate himself with people, forms, operations, nature, and other elements in the surrounding phenomena. Each one—with unique growth patterns and experiences, and with feelings, needs, habits, and inclinations—is involved in the process of "becoming" and being in the role of mankind. The experiences of each represent a way of living, working, and thinking together —yet in individually different directions. As we have seen, the child must be helped to locate himself with problems, issues, events, and relationships that invite reflective thought and may provide clues for his authentic identification with the role of mankind. The individual will find his locations through the invitation to meanings provided by key questions and the ideas that grow out of the questions. He will also locate himself with the relationship of meanings in the various subjects. This does not mean that the subjects have been prebuilt and "set" for all times and places. Rather, it means that the learner must have the opportunity to behave with the subject content in such a manner that he veritably moves with the structure of knowledge beyond any artificial boundaries.

Children should find identity as human beings as they relate to each other and to things. As children behave with items and conditions in the environment they become involved as human beings. Human feelings come into play as they talk about their involvements in such terms as, "I liked the feel of it," "I did not think much about it," "I thought I wouldn't like it," "It was fun and I would like to try it again," "It was different than I thought," "I never saw anything just like this," and others. Children also get involved with other children and adults. They are conscious about others and how they behave with things. They will find that others have some of the same experiences that they had.

Then too they will find that although others have viewed the same things, many will express themselves quite differently relative to the same experiences.

As children relate to things, ideas, and to each other they come to ponder and value the behavior of individual human beings as that behavior differs from child to child. These differences in behavior will bring into focus an expanded humanness in people as they detect different meanings in similar phenomena. This in turn will reveal to each one messages not originally within his purview. These messages suggest many meanings about humans. They suggest, for example, that each one from day to day encounters experiences which indicate much about one's behavior. Furthermore, the messages cause individuals to formulate ideas that will stimulate more attempts at probing about their behavior and what it does to their daily feelings about life and its meanings. In their awareness about behavior children make new discoveries about themselves.

As individuals relate to their surroundings they begin to gather ideas about why a human being behaves as he does. Also, they form ideas about how behavior changes as individuals grow older. They view the behavior of individuals who are younger and also those who have approached adulthood. Different individuals do many things over the years and also cause much to happen to themselves and to others. All are born, go through a life period of behavior, and come to an end. All living things go through a life cycle. This life cycle is the same for all living things—animals and plants—in that individuals in each group are born, grow, reproduce, and die.

One of the most fundamental and exciting approaches to greater meanings about man and what is human about him is found in some of the publications of the Educational Development Center, Inc., Cambridge, Massachusetts. The particular publication suggested here is *Man: A Course of Study* which is a one-year course for upper elementary grades developed by the Social Studies Program of Education Development Center. The broad outlines of this course were sketched by Jerome Bruner, Director of the Center for Cognitive Studies at Harvard University. He stated, "The content of the course is man: his nature as a species, the forces that shaped and continue to shape his humanity.... We seek exercises and materials which show wherein man is distinctive in his adaptation to the world, and wherein there is a discernible continuity between man and his forbears."[1] The course makes new demands on teachers. They will need to become students

---

[1] From Bulletin *Man: A Course of Study* (Cambridge, Mass.: Educational Development Center, Inc., 1969).

of new writing in the behavioral sciences. They meet situations in which questions arise which have no clear-cut answers. Teachers are challenged by issues such as reproduction, aggression, killing, religion, life and death in classroom discussion. Teachers will be in the position of first behavers in exploring new roles for themselves in the classroom.[2]

The publication suggested proposes and outlines a more useful and careful way of looking at data and relationships about man and what makes him human. The material has been carefully researched through authropological studies which provide most important clues to an understanding of the nature of man and how he behaves. It should indeed be intriguing to children and expand their relations to meanings and ideas about themselves and others.

Patterson, in the development of curriculum models for junior high school social studies, provides a most useful approach to man's behavior on a different theme than that just mentioned. The theme, *Man as a Political Being,* is designed for three courses roughly parallel to Grades 7, 8, and 9. In connection with this theme, he says,

> The focus provided . . . as we will see, is not narrow; with it we can scan a wide range, since man political is many things. The theme and its subordinate curriculum components are chosen because of what we know of the politicization process in individual development. From a free society's point of view, it is important for the child in early adolescence to be given as much opportunity as possible to develop his ability to think about public affairs and politics and to examine meaning and value in history and government. We chose this focus, too, because it appears—on the basis of observation and experiment—to excite the interest and engage the energies of children.[3]

In the confrontation of the teacher and child with themselves as political beings they should come into a working contact with many elements which tend to shape and involve them with their surroundings as human beings. They would relate to power, for example, and its association with governance. They would deal with power factors in play, work, corruption, and in other involvements as human beings. They would relate to all the fields of study in their attempts at probing for meanings about society and their part in it. The confrontations would extend to other factors such as role, status, system, culture, and the like.

In the attempt to relate to meanings and ideas about man and his behavior all areas should be probed for messages. Actually, this process becomes one of involvement and should not be contrived in terms of

[2] *Ibid.*
[3] Franklin Patterson, Curriculum Models for Junior High School Studies (Cambridge, Mass.: Educational Services Inc., 1965).

subject areas. In other words, one should not indulge a preoccupation with this subject or that one as being the one where entrance for probing about behavior should begin. It is important then to look at man, what he is, how he came to be, how is he different from his forebears and animals and then follow him into whatever area the inquiry leads us. The inquirer or behaver, whether teacher, pupil, or just anybody, should be *above* any of the plans and proposals yet at the same time *with* them.

Plans and proposals, other than those already mentioned, which suggest exciting sources and directions for inquiry are those being developed by the Anthropology Curriculum Study Project in Chicago, Ill. This project is sponsored by the American Anthropological Association and supported by the National Science Foundation. The experimental units developed are *The Study of Early Man, The Great Transformation,* and *On Studying Societies. The Study of Early Man* is described as having to do with the early career of our species, with man the hunter-gatherer. *The Great Transformation* focuses on the major cultural transformation triggered by the beginnings of agriculture: the growth of peasant and urban societies. Another unit, *Studying Societies,* provides a model for analyzing historical societies in anthropological terms and applies the model to the analysis of classical Greece. The units are designed for secondary school world history programs.[4]

Case studies of these units have been published and are now available.

Many other plans and proposals have been developed by other groups and are being tested in various schools over the country. The ones mentioned are representative of efforts by individuals and bodies to break out, so to speak, from the "settled" role of the social studies into a new vitality associated with man and his behavior as he extends his sense of being as a human. A limitation that somehow appears to persist in these efforts, however, is a sort of funneling into a school structure which perhaps should not exist in its present form anyway. Another limitation may be the zeal to put the ideas of the programs into "packages" for teachers and schools. The danger that persists in this connection may be the temptation on the part of some to superimpose the plans into the schools and thus have another institutionalized form. It is hoped that these issues will be most carefully considered by both the bodies which are at work producing the programs and those associated with systems that will use them.

Children might identify authentic realities in topics or questions

[4]*Anthropology Curriculum StudysProject Newsletter,* No. 4, Anthropology Curriculum Study Project, 5632 Kimbark Avenue, Chicago, Ill. (Fall 1965) pages.

which may be involved with the social studies and the arts. The various items of content of each subject must, of course, be dealt with in isolation from time to time to clarify certain points and emphasize some aspects peculiar to the subject. This is done, however, mainly to enable children to acquire a sense of wholeness of meaning in relating one item to another. Care should be taken, however, that the separation does not keep meanings in compartments out of relation to one another. To illustrate this in social studies let's consider the study of food. Food is read about, talked about, and then various concepts are established relative to its origin, where it is found, how it is distributed and so on. The topic of food, in other words, is dealt with separately and, although some facts and meanings are established, there is a rather constricted approach if any to related meanings.

Meanings about food come to be associated with it, and inventiveness of people in processing and distributing it. Research "in miniature" could be carried on with children to show the relative activities of men, women, and children with the acquisition of food. For example, instead of visiting a grocery store to establish facts about what is there, children would be encouraged to observe the work different people do there, including the customer and the type of knowledge needed by these people. Furthermore, children might secure simple data about behavior of people in selecting food in a supermarket and the possible reasons for this behavior. They might, also, make checks at different hours to determine whether the proportion of women shoppers to men shoppers changes.

Other questions on the topic of food might relate to packaging, the relationship of abundance to population and the relation of abundance to geographical areas. Some simple approaches could be designed to encourage inquiry into man's ingenuity to create the abundance already suggested. Furthermore, simple concepts could be developed with respect to the necessity of related occupations and research to provide food. Still further areas of inquiry could be in the behavior of people with food in families, in restaurants and so on.

More searching questions relative to the topic of food would relate to the problems of adequate supply to all people. It has been suggested above that man possesses great ability to produce food in abundance and to distribute it. Does this mean then that no one remains hungry? Obviously the question needs no answer. There are millions of people throughout the world who are literally starving—in the United States as well as in other nations. The question might be phrased, In a world where abundance is prevalent, why does hunger still exist? This question, of course, poses a paradoxical situation—abundance and hunger existing virtually side by side.

In approaching this question, there must develop some real confrontation with present realities. These evoke the whole question of man's inhumanity to man. The problems of the economy must come under severe scrutiny. The values basic to this problem must be laid bare. Why do individuals and systems permit a condition where children grow up unhealthy because of hunger? Isn't this a form of violence? Doesn't the continuation of this condition among many people suggest a callous indifference to the birthright of human beings? How are we part of this problem?

It is important to develop the conditions where knowledge about deprivation must be internalized and translated into immediate action. The topic of food and its relation to individuals and their values takes on meaning with respect to humanization. The ingredients of the existing realities must be brought into sharp focus through intensive inquiry. The whole question of poverty and deprivation here may take on dimensions not previously conceived. To be sure, poverty prevails in many places. In this conception of poverty one may assume the attitude of immunity to it especially if he views himself as being in the affluent area. This is a form of detachment which may put one out of a sense of awareness to some basic questions about human concern. Again, it is necessary to refer to the importance of an individual's recognition and admission that he is part of the problem he is trying to solve—in this case, poverty and deprivation. Isn't he deprived when he detaches himself from his part in the perpetuation of the poverty conditions? Isn't the affluent one building pockets of deprivation when he accepts the affluent conditions without assessing their ingredients? The indifference and out-of-awareness which may follow as one detaches himself from the elements of causation of poverty is in itself a definite form of deprivation residing in him. One is indeed deprived if he is unable to confront the poverty pockets both in the condition of affluence and in the lack of it.

In seeking a location in the role of mankind or the extension of one's existence, multiple points of inquiry are necessary for the development of meanings. Thus it is important that there be extended emphasis with usual topics. In the approach to meanings about the home and family we must consider how a family is a part of one's existence, how and why one fulfills certain responsibilities, and the nature of one's identity with the home. The realities about the home and family will then be extended into a sense of behavior which suggests more than a completed fact.

As children begin to detect the meaning of the roles of the different members of a family, they will extend their existence through new opportunities which will be conceived in the family unit. They begin to form concepts about such intangibles as love, sacrifice, belonging, care, and other relationships. They become more cognizant of the uniqueness of the individual family members, not in terms of tangible elements alone but in terms of the pursuit of being. They value the individuals not in terms of possessing a list of qualities but in seeking an expression of self. What frequently is referred to as *home and family* as an instructional unit becomes a whole area of relationships with being, and a condition of gaining messages about existence which point beyond immediate fulfillment characterized by the expressions "to get along" or "to learn to live with one another."

Children extend their sense of existence as they relate to their life space. In order to help generate the conditions for expanded meanings teachers should help bring into the learning situations those elements to which children might relate as they move in their life space. Books and other materials should be made accessible to enable children to relate their experiences with their reading and forms of expression. All the contacts children have experienced in terms of their viewing of areas of interest, their observations in museums, galleries, their reactions to people whom they have encountered, and their readings will contribute to the extension of their life space. The classroom and school should provide direction to the media through which children as individuals might represent both their observed and projected meanings relative to this expanding life space. The individual child should have the opportunity to locate himself with respect to his expanding needs and existence. By locating himself is meant the points of contact where he finds both a degree of comfort and spontaneity in pursuing meanings. This would also be the place where he has identity.

As different individuals represent their locations through all media of expression, there should develop a confrontation with a variety of meanings as the differences are noted. Out of this could come a sense of wisdom relative to the versatility employed by individuals in pursuing needs which may in fact be similar. It would be obvious to the imaginative person that in this form of inquiring and facilitation of being, the arts would not only need to come into play but would also give individual direction to greater existence. By existence here is meant the employment as well as the generation of resources to approach some dimensions of authentic reality. Putting it another way, although the employment of the arts would suggest a dimension of immediate idea representation, they would be used to suggest an individual's feeling about truth and beauty which provides a sense of fulfillment in itself.

Man's pursuit of greater wisdom in the arts is related to his survival in the natural environment, but in this very relationship man moves into an expanded sense of existence. Children never have in mind the idea of survival, nor should they. Instead, they see and hear interesting things, people, media, and happenings. They are sensitive to almost everything around them as a form of actualization. They are curious and want to touch, move, paint, look, and like. Children look with wonderment at surrounding phenomena and should be encouraged to express it in their own way. In that expression would be so much truth and meaning that the greatness of it would give strength to the understanding individual. It is in this sense that the design of the pursuit of inquiry by the individual and his associates would enable him to approach more closely the eternal "answers" to Who am I? What am I? Why am I here? Where am I going? What is within my reach? How do I take hold of it? What can be seen? What remains unseen? As the child works with his sketch book, for example, he begins to represent feelings and meanings relative to these and other questions. He will sketch objects and ideas not necessarily related to these questions. He will try to use media other than paper and the sketch book to represent objects and ideas as they convey meaning to him. He may put them in wood, metal, soap, or words. Some child may even begin to work with stone. He may make movies. Children will be the artists employing the media of painting, carving, and sculpturing in promoting or designing the ingredients of being and greater existence. Children are then constantly finding and employing more resources and media to approach a greater feeling of authentic reality.

The behavior inherent in the preceding discussion and illustrations is representative of the thinking not only of the children but also of the teacher and his associates. As a teacher begins to consider answers to basic questions he too must feel a sense of direction toward greater authenticity. He will then behave in such a way as to generate conditions that will develop a compulsiveness in children to employ surrounding resources, and detect connections toward new meanings and resources. Out of this will come a continuous accretion of representations of realities. Children will create extended realities with their paintings, statuary, sculpturing, music, and other media of representation.

An individual employs the arts in association with other areas to generate meanings and ideas about human behavior. One behaves as he relates to the content of subject areas. This behavior is revealed through various forms of expression the least of which are not the arts. Yet too frequently and too universally the arts are viewed as appendages to twhat is regarded as the "realistic" substance or functional content in instructional programs. This observation becomes more obvious when one views much of the thinking associated with the development of so-called affirmations about realization. Reference here is to such statements as the following: "Man has learned to survive in his environment." "Man finds new ways to improve his relationships with his environment." "Man's acts evolve from and influence his total way of life." Other statements would suggest the importance of the whole child, the question of an integrated personality, and the development of a many-sided individual. All of these affirmations, are related to the importance of a sense of individual realization and fulfillment. The statements, however, seem to point to an after-the-fact development of an individual. They suggest that one needs to do many things to reach the end. For example, one statement contends that man has learned to survive. One might raise the question, Isn't it just as important to survive so that he will learn? Isn't it just as important to learn so that he will survive? Isn't learning the same as an extended existence? With the conditions for greater existence he transcends survival as he makes his mind. An individual does not learn first and survive later but the act of learning continues and is expanded with survival. The arts, as well as other areas should supersede or at least be an accompanying experience with survival rather than be appended to it after the fact. Man behaves with the act of survival rather than before or after the act. Since behavior proceeds simultaneously with expression, substance or so-called content cannot be separated from that expression. Expression and behavior become a unity in the act of existence and authentic reality. A beautiful package is just as real to a child as the gift inside, and the color in a painting is just as real to him as the elements of the composition.

In the statement "Man finds new ways to improve his relationships with his environment" the thinking seems to suggest that one has to first find or discover and then relate. On the contrary, isn't it more true that an individual relates and finds at the same time? Here again, since behavior and expression are a unity, the arts find and relate at one and the same time. Thus the arts are equally the substance of existence and reality as any other area such as social studies or mathematics. The applicable theory here is that man employs the arts along with other areas of content in providing for himself the contact points that facilitate his sense of integrity with his environment. There exists then no hierarchy of subject matters through which he promotes his existential fulfillment.

The employment of the arts in providing contact points for meaning suggests some extremely important revelations about how individual behaviors have been formed. In an earlier section it was suggested that the arts have been lumped under other areas such as social studies and science, and then only as appendages. This clearly indicates a way of behavior which reveals some questionable choices on the part of certain individuals. For example, for these individuals the arts are set-tled for as "having a place" in the curriculum. This attitude clearly reveals a sense of values which assumes thinking about the so-called hard disciplines as having priority over the arts in the program of learn-ing. One wonders why those who entertain this attitude (and there are too many who do) would include art at all. There may be several reasons for admitting art at all in the program of learning. One reason for this reluctance is the lack of awareness of the relentless efforts of artists to give real voice to the expression of man's destiny and direction. Another reason for including it in the program of studies may be to show evi-dence that it is well for people to have some interest in "culture." Still others would include art in the curriculum for those who have "artistic talent" and for some students who need an extra half credit or so to graduate. Then there are individuals (not enough of them) who feel that the arts are "real" and will help those who are associated with the other disciplines to extend their sense of authentic reality in their relation to the world.

The arts are indeed central to all the disciplines. As one seriously views natural phenomena one stands in awe about the sculpture that is evolved in so many shapes and forms. As we view the efforts of the painter, we cannot help but be moved by the struggle to give expression and meaning to man and events. As an individual becomes more in-volved with the thought and struggles of the painter, he is beginning to relate himself to the *what is* and to see the distinction between the regularity of systems and the *real*. McLuhan[5] speaks of the arts as prophetic and suggests that they enable us to discover social and psychic targets in plenty of time to prepare to cope with them. The arts are much more than the popular conception as mere self-expression.

Dewey, in his own incomparable manner, has given a rather plau-sible explanation for the rather meager position art has occupied in education when he states,

> It is by way of communication that art becomes the incomparable organ of instruction, but the way is so remote from that usually as-sociated with the idea of education, it is a way that lifts art so far above what we are accustomed to think of as instruction, that we are repelled by any suggestion of teaching and learning in connection with art. . . . Our revolt is in fact a reflection upon education that proceeds by methods so literal as to exclude the imagination and one not touching the desires and emotions of men.[6]

Dewey emphasizes the unique quality of art by stating that "art is more

[5]Marshal McLuhan, *Understanding Media* (New York: Signet Books, 1964), p. xi.
[6]John Dewey, *Art as Experience* (New York: Putnam, 1958), p. 347.

moral than moralities."[7] He suggests that moralities tend to become consecrations of the status quo, reflections of custom, and reenforcements of the established order. "The moral prophets of humanity," he says, "have always been poets even though they spoke in free verse or by parable."[8] Their vision of possibilities, however, has soon been codified as facts that already exist and are hardened into forms of institutionalization. Dewey suggests that art has seemed to keep alive the sense of purposes that outrun evidence and of meanings that transcend indurated habit.[9]

The arts just do not lend themselves to arrangement into existent facts. They are over and beyond this type of treatment. They stand by themselves to convey an unvarnished reality as to *what is*. It is important that individuals develop an openness in which their senses become lucid to the vital messages which the arts are so plainly communicating. It is indeed most significant that individuals engaged in education are first behavers in developing the conditions for artists to be brought into the mainstream of the disciplines—not to be appropriated but to actually be the real disciplinarians in the quest for knowledge. As we listen to the clarion call of the artist, we will indeed detect in him the harbinger of things to come.

As the painter struggles to give meaning and events largely through the medium of color and detail, so does the poet give meaning through sound and language. The musician blends his thought and feeling with the poet as he portrays the human quest. The novelist struggles to convey messages about the human condition, about the quest for meaning, the search for the real, the authentic. The dramatist depicts man in his anguished state and his search for greater existence. The arts are by no means confined to the poet, the painter, the novelist, the men of literature. They extend to the scientist, the mathematician, the historian, the philosopher, the sociologist and to all engaged in inquiry through the many media and disciplines. In this relation with the various disciplines the arts are obviously more than associate elements. The artist may be the scientist, the historian, the physicist, the social scientist—and vice versa.

A word of caution on the whole question of relating to this or that area is in order. There is a tendency to relate in terms of the constituted academic disciplines. To do this may be a sort of hangup in that one may find oneself compelled to relate to meanings which somehow are irrelevant. There might be an absence of that sense of release essential to true

---

[7] *Ibid.*, p. 348.
[8] *Ibid.*, p. 348.
[9] *Ibid.*, p. 348.

adventure with meanings. Perhaps individuals could better reach a true relationship to meanings by approaching the question of how things are without any compulsion to begin with a discipline. For example, one may wish to examine the implications in the statement "That is the way it is." Some questions that might arise here are, Is this a way of saying that we should not think further? What is one talking or thinking about when one says this? Does it suggest that we cannot possibly find out how things really are?

A point which seems to be strongly suggested by these questions is that further probing may require an approach quite different than in the comfort or confinement of social studies, mathematics, or some other familiar subject. The approach would suggest a deviation from the thinking associated with going through this or that area in order to relate to ideas on how things are. Actually the idea of "going through" science, social studies, the arts or other areas suggests a narrowing of inquiry by the elimination of alternatives. It suggests that thinking of men is confined to an established order of knowledge. It might further indicate an attitude that thinking outside of this order is capricious. In this attitude one is always looking as to where *this* can be done rather than doing it. There is a tendency to look somewhere else even if what one is thinking about may be within one's immediate reach.

In relating oneself to broad questions such as those concerned with how things are, it may be necessary to separate from the behaviors normally carried on so as to become cognizant about them. This approach is in accord with the approach suggested in the first chapter. Care should be taken that one does this for the purpose of ascertaining the types of behaviors exhibited in the notion of "how things are" rather than as an academic exercise. The question actually is associated with many other questions which have been thought about by men in other times and places. Furthermore, it is related to all the disciplines. A probing on the question would have the effect of transforming and extending the disciplines as well as the ones who do the probing. This could come about as individual teachers and children would confront the behaviors associated with the questions of how things are. Individuals could begin to confront their behaviors in carrying through with the *what is*. They would begin to discern the rationalities of the *what is* along with the absurdities and questionable assumptions underlying some of the behavior with it. They would try to discern some of the common as well as varied substance of established patterns of behavior with the way things are.

The questions that arise as individuals inquire into the way things are become quite involved. Some might relate to the relevant and irrelevant behaviors in teaching. When one says to a child "I will teach you

...," does he proceed irrespective of the child's need for involvement? Has he tried to ascertain how the child possibly is already doing in his own way that which he is to be taught? Is there a clear invitation to the one to be taught to make himself known? Is the teacher listening? Is he hearing? Is he making himself aware of what is happening? A sensitivity to these questions could bring into focus some ideas relative to *what is.* There may appear some signs of thoughtful response to the issues. Individual children may be developing media to relate their responses to their thinking. Some individuals no doubt may indicate their anguished state with respect to their captivation with respect to certain teaching routines. Some may express their thoughts and feelings in poetry. Others may relate their experiences in aphorisms. Still others may develop models through sculpturing. Many may use the various media of the fine arts by painting, drawing, and other forms to give meaning to their thoughts.

In relating to their meanings, some children may express the denial of the quest for involvement by indicating the nature of human despair through varied media. Some may depict relevances to their sense of existence. Having sensed the *what is*, they will tend to point the way. Having confronted with various questions with a sense of history, some individuals will tend to release their thinking through literature. They will represent themselves through prose, poetry, drama, and other art forms. Various individuals may seek a confrontation with extended existence through music. The novel will find its way to some individuals as an art form for authentic confrontation with extended existence.

There is a tendency in discourse of this type and with this substance to act as if this has to happen in a school between teacher and student. If this type of confined thinking seems to follow on the part of the individual, it may be useful for him to actually approach this as a question of *what is* so as to confront some of the absurdities present. It is important for one to separate himself from himself so that his mind may become lucid to this condition of closure and captivity. A teacher may become an artist when he transcends school and any other institution to confront the way of the authentic. This does not mean that he absents himself from school or other institutions. Such a condition would be captivity in reverse.

The arts are always productive of predicaments for those who would become involved with them. The way of comfort and solution resides in the arrangements of the closed system which are discussed in another chapter. These arrangements usually demand conditions of confinement such as are found in rigid institutionalism. The role there is occupied with the solutions of problems, which may be another way of saying that learning is a form of escape from any confrontation with the real. Although the one who is involved with the arts is in anguish with the predicament, he finds true being in the confrontation with it. The predicament is, in fact, the curriculum of the true artist. It is a condition where all his senses are brought into play to relate to meanings which hold relevance to him and others for greater existence. As he becomes more human, he will produce more predicaments which in turn invite him to discover ever new elements for human elevation. In the predicaments he will realize, perhaps, one of the great quests of human being—that of greater involvement, not only with more points of contact productive of ideas but also with peculiar or unique dimensions of relevant conditions for the approach to the authentic.

As implied in the above discussion a rather prevalent and unexamined condition and process in learning is drive reduction—the resolving of predicaments. This condition is neither realistic nor adequate when one examines carefully how children and young people seek relevant meanings to extend their sense of existence. This is true also of adults in their efforts to inquire into knowledge. It seems imperative then to reconsider the usual concept of competence. This becomes quite apparent as one observes the play experiences of contented children. They crave stimulation. They seem to thrive on novelty and the opportunity to deal with the problematic. Interest requires elements of unfamiliarity. They not only create predicaments for themselves but enter with great excitement into the task of extracting meanings from them. They do not settle on these meanings but probe further for something still to be found out and for something else still to be learned. Granted that the climate of inquiry is present, children and young people put themselves into question and actually produce predicaments where an optimal level of uncertainty is present. The level of curiosity becomes extended as they respond to uncertainty and ambiguity. They approach discrepant events and discontinuous conditions with real thought and firm determination.

As children bring their senses into play in individual ways of inquiry, they not only use media which are accessible and relevant but build new media and art forms. Through these media and art forms they appropriate meanings for the extension of themselves. Young children who have encountered the conditions of release for meanings will not only play in the sand but will use the sand to be a relevant medium for the extension of their being. They will not only represent the facts of regular existence but will create new and extended meanings toward extended possibilities. They will build roads that lead to someone and to somewhere. As a result of their valuing about the someone or somewhere, they will come back and improve and even redevelop the roads.

The roads to them must not only become the avenues to friends but invite friends to redevelop the routes to an extended sense of inquiry about human elevation.

The conditions for testing these theories would involve intensive observation as to the manner in which children locate themselves with meanings and ideas in their domain of being. Furthermore, the observations of children should also ascertain how they expand their domain of being. By domain here is meant the range of relationships developed as children relate to meanings and ideas. The hypotheses relative to locating with and expanding the domains of children could be derived from theorizing about how they might be influenced by this or that area or experience in the approach to meanings. Some children may relate mainly through what might be considered as the social studies. Others would be helped to relate through mathematics, still others through the arts, and so on.

Variations to the process of relating to a domain would be developed through interrelationships between two or more areas, and also shifting the areas used over a period of time into other combinations of relationships. The observer could be the teacher or others, who would try to determine on the basis of criteria indicative of extending relationships of ideas, through which type or types of inquiry the individual domain of being would most nearly be fulfilled. For fear that someone may construe a theory and its testing as another *core* or *unified studies* approach, we hasten to say that this is not intended. No effort will be made here to place the process of relating to meanings into this or that system. Rather, the relating to meanings is to be pursued through the separate areas, using other areas as media to extend conceptual realizations in the separate areas. Hypotheses which might be considered for testing the theories indicated might be as follows: The approach to meanings through the arts will extend the location points of learning of the child in his domain at least to the same degree as when the approach is made through any other area. The approach to meanings through the social studies will extend the location points of the child in his domain to the same degree as when the approach is made through the arts, and vice versa. When the approach to meanings is made through relating social studies to the arts, the degree of extension of the child in his domain is no greater than if the approach is through the arts alone. The approach to meanings through mathematics alone will show a lesser degree of extension of the child in his domain than if phases of the arts are included in the approach. In the approach to meanings through the area of mathematics alone the child will be less extended in his domain than in any one of the areas of social studies, science, reading, or the arts.

The type of hypothesizing suggested is not exhaustive relative to the theories. The hypotheses as stated are simply to suggest possible ways in which one or more individuals may think about ways of expanding the experiential domains of children. More important is to think of ways by which children themselves expand their domains. Other individuals in hypothesizing on the extension of location places for meanings for young children may relate to entirely different subjects or topics or combinations of subjects or topics. Furthermore, their experiences with idea development in content would differ from one to another. One individual's way of expanding his domain of experiences and ideas may have been through the subject of science or arithmetic, while another was occupied in this expansion with the area of language development. Still other individuals may have devoted their efforts in gaining meanings by observations with topics such as transformation of plants in growth, the behavior of people in certain circumstances, the nature of love and its workings with people, the idea of even and odd, the question of symmetry in a culture, the changes in a community over the past five years and the accompanying related behavior. Some individuals may probe the electronic environment for relevant meanings. No doubt the different individuals would establish different hypotheses in their quest to develop location places for meanings not only for themselves but also with others.

It is important that the hypothesizer be the first behaver in developing theories and testing them. At the same time other individuals around him are also being first behavers in thinking through with their theories and proceeding to test them. Elements of significance relative to different theories about extending the conditions for the development of meanings would become apparent to the individual behavers, especially if there existed that "openness to experience" characterized by the trust of the mind. Individuals would then enter into conversation or dialogue regarding their theories. This confrontation would tend to relate to the thinking of many minds and thus expand the capacity of individual minds to move into alternative procedures relative to theory and instructional conditions. The conditions for extraction of mind should have the invitational ingredients for all in the instructional setting. Under these conditions children would not only be first behavers in developing theories and hypotheses for testing them in their own way but would also be in dialogue with adults in these efforts.

As an individual proceeds to test his theory with children in their efforts at inquiry he will begin to ask questions about his practices and the conditions which he has set up for inquiry stations to develop. More important, he will begin to evaluate his dimensions of understanding and beliefs relative to the purposes of education. An important factor here would be to assess the purposes of education in terms of the domains of experience and meanings of children. A teacher naturally will theorize with respect to achievement on the part of children as they respond to various areas of study. As one becomes involved in a setting where theory is being experienced, he should begin to receive and decipher the messages relative to what is usually considered as achievement. In transforming these messages he will begin to feel the importance of formulating new theory which should eventute into expanded meanings and relationships. This presents a rather challenging problem relative to the definition of and conditions for expanded relationships. He will think about and help children think about the experiences in terms of what they did to them—where they led them.

Whenever one regards his experiences in terms of where they led him he is thinking of the consequences of the experiences. He then predicts the consequences in similar experiences. He forms abstractions from the experiences. This is one way in which he extends his definition of himself. In defining himself—that is, in discerning what structures of meaning he brings around himself—he may begin to ask some questions. He may ask, "In my prediction of consequences through similar experiences, have I separated myself from other possible facts and meanings?" "Have I settled on a certain route of inquiry thus cutting myself off from other routes?" "Have I regarded and confronted the meanings of other individuals as I have proceeded to extend my realities?" "Have I developed a hierarchy in relating to knowledge, thus excluding vital subject matter?"

The whole question of extending one's realities through defining oneself is related to the thinking surrounding the hypotheses indicated previously. Hypotheses result from theories arising from one's threshold of knowledge. Accordingly, the theories and hypotheses may be slanted in terms of one's areas of knowledge. To describe this it is necessary to note again the nature of the hypotheses stated earlier. It will be noted that the hypotheses regarding learners' locations with meanings suggested that these locations will tend to be extended when the approach is through the arts, social studies, reading, or science. A single exception seemed to be the hypotheses relating to the approach through mathematics. It was hypothesized that when an approach to the development of extended realities was made through mathematics alone there would be a lesser degree of identification of the learner with meaning locations than when places of the arts are included in the approach. It was further hypothesized that this will also be true in the approach respectively through social studies, science, reading, or the arts. The nature of the hypothesizing would suggest that the teacher or whoever was proposing the hypotheses may have been less knowledgeable in mathematics than in the other areas indicated. It is possible that his experiences with mathematics were either lacking or were of such a nature that they did not lead him to knowledge in this area. Certainly what knowledge he did have in the mathematics area may not have provided extended experiences for multiple locations with meanings in it. What is even more important, his experiences with mathematics did not influence him in bringing his experiences in the other subject matter areas to bear on his occupation with mathematics.

What has been indicated about the hypotheses above is associated with initial theory development—prior to the attempts at testing the theory. The range and intensity of an individual's identity with meanings relative to a content area is determined by the definition of his existence with the area. As a person proceeds to prepare the ground for testing the hypotheses and the theories relative to a rather limited encounter with a field of study he may, thereby, be constricting his own inquiry as well as that of the learners relative to it. In his efforts then to develop theories and hypotheses relative to the pursuit of an area of study he should extend his inquiry into other fields so that he can extract related aspects of knowledge from those fields. At the same time he will be bringing his theories into relationship with others so that he can lend strength to their areas of study. Theorizing in which one extends his encounter to many areas of content other than his own will tend to transform and expand those areas even as he is transformed into a more human condition.

At this point the avid researcher would proceed to develop criteria as to the possible extent of the domain within which learners would find location places with meanings. The researcher, who may be the teacher in this case, would carry through with the testing of the hypotheses on the basis of the criteria established relative to the domain of meanings. This procedure suffers from several limitations. In the first place, the procedure would be predicated on the assumption that the researcher was cognizant of the extent of the domain of the learners' thinking about, and relating to, knowledge. This may be a questionable and precarious assumption. In the second place, the procedure would be based on the idea that the hypotheses were settled postulations. It is obvious that this attempt would be a condition of sidestepping some important alternatives or shifts in the hypotheses. The matter of rushing into a procedure to test hypotheses may reduce rather than extend meanings. This would suggest that the most productive activity on the part of both the teacher and pupils may be to ask questions in terms of the thinking that gave rise to the hypotheses. The most productive development of criteria for an extended domain of location areas with meaning would be to examine the thinking routes which led to the establishment of certain hypotheses. Herein would lie the ground for the development of subject-matter content through which the learners as well as the teachers would find expanded fields of identification.

In view of the thinking indicated in the sections above, the whole matter of hypothesizing takes on great importance in the approach to extended realities in all the content areas. The testing of hypotheses would retain its usefulness in the development of the conditions for extended meanings. The testing, however, would not become a type of door-closing act to meanings such as may be associated with the restatement of hypotheses only after the testing was completed. Rather, it would be involved with the questions raised by the learners as to why they had arrived at certain hypotheses. These questions may reveal certain gaps in theorizing which would lead to the need for different hypotheses. In this condition, before any alternative hypotheses would be established the learners would have to become involved in the key questions of subject-matter content. This would have the effect of developing new location places with meanings on the part of children and adults.

SELECTED READINGS

Bruner, Jerome S. *Toward a Theory of Instruction.* Cambridge, Mass.: Harvard U. P., 1966.

Educational Development Center, Inc. *Man: A Course of Study.* Cambridge, Mass., 1965–69.

Galbraith, Kenneth. *Liberal Hour.* Boston: Houghton, 1960.

Kuh, Katharine. "The Art Education Myth," *Saturday Review,* Sept. 28, 1968, pp. 50-53.

Lampman, Archibald. "The Clearer Self," *Unseen Wings: The Living Poetry of Man's Immorality.* New York: Beechhurst Press, 1949.

McLuhan, Marshall. *Understanding Media.* New York: Signet Books, 1964, p. 11.

Malraux, André. *Museum Without Walls.* Vol. I of *Psychology of Art.* New York: Pantheon, 1949-51.

Maslow, Abraham (ed.). *New Knowledge in Human Values.* New York: Harper, 1965, pp. 137-151.

Michael, Donald N. *The Next Generation: The Prospects Ahead for the Youth of Today and Tomorrow.* New York: Vintage Books, 1963.

Patterson, Franklin. *Curriculum Models for Junior High School Studies.* Cambridge, Mass.: Educational Services, Inc., 1965.

Randall, John Herman. *The Role of Knowledge in Western Religion.* Boston: Beacon Press, 1958.

Teilhard de Chardin, Pierre. *The Phenomenon of Man.* New York: Harper, 1959.

chapter 7

On Inquiry with Youth and Older Learners

All learners young and old approach meanings through content which is more or less similar in nature. The meanings that are derived, however, are not the same for each individual. It has been suggested that all knowledge be brought into the purview of the child at a very early age. This is done in terms of how a child looks at his world and how he defines it for himself. It is reasonable to assume that as the child advances in years he encounters experiences that continue to alter the manner in which he perceives the world. No doubt the world and the environment in which the child has his experiences somehow present different meanings to him at almost every step of his growth to youth and adulthood. As the youth looks back at what to him seem many years, he senses the changes that have taken place around him and to some degree takes cognizance of those changes in terms of what they have done to him as an individual. At the same time he may contemplate what has happened and try to look at what might happen in the years to come.

There seems to be a great deal of rhetorical thinking about the inevitability of change. The whole question of change is verbalized so much, especially in education literature, that it appears to be viewed as a settled condition. Inherent in this thinking is that any change somehow moves people and conditions forward and upward. Also inherent in this thinking is that the means used or encountered in this movement will cause an individual to grow from lesser to more, from childhood to manhood, from immaturity to maturity, and so on. Somehow it is assumed that as one grows older, knowledge will follow as an accumulative attribute with that growth.

Viewing the whole question of developing expanded realities with learners, we should give due attention to the matter of what happens to an individual as he grows from infancy to adulthood. Incidental to this matter is a careful recall and consideration of "moments" which have been felt as relevant to one's development. By "moments" here is meant those happenings which somehow stood out for an individual. By considering what is happening to him now, the individual has to put himself into relation with the influences which have seemed important to him as he was growing up.

In considering the moments of his existence, one puts oneself into question. As an individual is trying to ascertain those experiences or happenings which have at different times seemed relevant to him, he has to be in question. Otherwise the relevances would not be intelligible to him, since they would not be pursued for their particular ingredients. To him the significance does not lie only in the fact that he was party to a change, but also in the effect the change had on his behavior as he approached the future. As Maslow[1] points out, each individual has his future within him now as of this moment, and it is incumbent on him to become conversant with the events of his existence so as to discern the present state of his being. What happened to him in the course of his becoming is still present now.

To enter into relation necessitates a thoughtful occupation with what are usually conceived of as realities. As a person puts himself into question, he drives toward questions about the nature of these realities. This involves some rather penetrating inquiry into the assumptions underlying the realities. He tries to determine the nature of the arrangements of the realities and how he is involved with them. Since he is in question he attempts to ascertain his behavior in the scheme of things as they are. As he views himself in question, he separates himself from the realities so that he might discern their effects on him. He then becomes the philosopher as well as the poet. He also helps others to become philosophers and poets through the means of confrontation in dialogue. Philosophy and art become the here and now of his existence. As the psalmist, he tends to look to the fields as they are ripe unto the harvest and to "look to the hills from which cometh his strength." He views all knowledge as being in his presence. He thus opens himself to this presence so that he might receive. As the poet and artist he opens himself to the world so that it will reveal its secrets to him.

As the individual in his state of separation becomes the poet, he begins to confront the meanings of his existence. As he relates himself to the moments of his becoming as well as the substance with which he has been and is now involved, he may begin to ascertain some of the different characteristics that have contributed to his sense of existence.

---

[1]Abraham H. Maslow, *Toward a Psychology of Being* (Princeton, N.J.: Van Nostrand, 1962), pp. 14–15.

In this relation he will begin to see some lineal experiences as well as configurative experiences which have been involved in his becoming. By lineal here is meant the experiences which appeared to have a certain sequential or step-by-step arrangement in the evolvement of meanings.

An example of a linear influence is the failure of an individual to recognize the error of the result of a computation without going through the steps of it. Another example would be where one would buy land indiscriminately to expand his possessions. This would be a situation where one would fail to take into account the total factors, ecological or otherwise, which tended to appreciate or depreciate its potential importance. The external organization of a certain number of courses or credit hours as requisites for graduation is based on linear concepts relative to learning. The programming of students through sixteen or so sequentially arranged units in a course in chemistry, biology, or some other subject constitutes a linear arrangement. The perusal of the materials and completion of requirements such as tests, projects, and so on is equated with finishing the course. The linear approach to meanings rests on the assumption that to learn anything properly, he should start from the "beginning." The "beginning" is usually preconceived by a teacher, textbook writer, or possibly another kind of program developer. The assumption here, which may be questionable, is that there is a beginning, a middle, and an ending to almost every form of discourse or study.

By configurations of meanings is meant a composite of relationships in which no discernible arrangement can be detected by the individual as he approaches the meanings. For example, a poem or painting may affect the behavior of an individual without his sensing or wishing to sense the reason for it. Professor Raymond Houghton refers to the individual's confrontation with configurations of meanings as mosaic thinking, as contrasted with lineal thinking. This suggests that the confrontation with meanings may be at any point and does not follow any sequential arrangement. The beginnings to ideas may be found at one or several points in the substance of subject matter or content encountered.

Whoever enters into knowledge with himself confronts himself as the predicament. It is actually impossible for him then to view himself as a lineal product. True, he cannot separate himself from many lineal conditions, but he does not find completion in those conditions. He will, however, always retain a sense of continuity with linear experiences because they are part of him as the question. The closed system of inquiry is always linear. It codifies all thought into lineal arrangements.

Realities are seen as regularized forms. Predicaments are encountered with regularized approaches for the purpose of eliminating them. Predicaments are not viewed as relevant to meanings in themselves but rather as outside of them.

In the open approach to meanings the individual is in a predicament and finds relevance in that condition. In the involvement with himself as the predicament he opens himself to more and more messages which then become relevant to his existence. He never removes himself out of the predicament but in his search for meanings he becomes associated with increasing numbers of predicaments. He encounters a mosaic of meanings in every predicament. The making of himself is a mosaic constellation of relationships. As the artist, he has to be in continuity with lineal arrangements, but goes into another dimension to become aware to *what is*. The *what is* is a configuration of meanings from which he derives meanings to further his sense of existence. As he inquires into the *what is*, his mind will become lucid to the ingredients which reside in this condition and he will then be in the position to make choices toward his expanded state of being.

The individual who has put himself into question begins to extract meanings from the substance in the surrounding phenomena. As he relates to his environment, he obviously will find relevant elements there with which he can come to a sense of integrity. He begins to make himself as he begins to make sense out of much of the substance with which he is involved. He thus encounters different elements of content which evolve as he drives toward the questions about his existence. Since he is in question, he generates relationships with the phenomena that surround him as a human being. The phenomena then become areas of content which seem to take shape and form as he puts himself into relation with them. He may, for example, view with increasing clarity the nature of his past experiences and to extract the influences which have tended to produce him as this particular human being. This actually puts him into a sense of history about his development, which in turn will put him into relation with events. Being in question, he would tend to surround himself with the motivations which he perceived as present in his involvement with his history. As he would involve himself more and more in history, he would begin to associate himself with the quest of human beings as they related themselves to historical movements. He would also come to a sense of realization of what happened to people in history, and what happened to history as people reacted to its events.

As one views the preceding discourse, it may appear to suffer from presumptuous reasoning in suggesting that the experiences implied will be automatic. This impression is not intended. The types of behavior suggested cannot be automatic when the behaver or behavers are in question. If one puts himself into question and is himself the predicament, he cannot help behaving in some respects in the manner indicated. The behaver becomes motivated as he views himself variously as a predicament and not a predicament. If the individual does not choose to put himself in question, it would follow that his contact with his surroundings would have no appreciable effect on him. True, there would obviously have to be some reaction but this would be passive. He would sidestep its effects. He would arrange himself in terms of it and then put it out of mind. All his efforts would be directed to a solution so that he could escape from it. As he puts himself into question, however, he returns to his surrounding phenomena to ascertain their ingredients so that he will attain a sense of awareness to their effects on him. He makes himself open to the content of the phenomena. Then, as the poet or artist, he appropriates selective elements of his surroundings to produce himself into a more authentic existence. What is more, he changes the surroundings so that the content in them will be expanded into new shapes and forms for his further illumination as a human being.

The condition indicated above may come about when an individual becomes so immersed in a discipline that he becomes immune to it. As the individual who is in question relates himself to history, he will find himself in a state of intimate relationship with much of the content of that subject. As he inquires further into the relationships of particular content, he will increasingly find himself involved in the discipline. He may, however, reach a saturation point in his involvement with a particular discipline, such as history. If he continues to pursue the content even after he has reached the saturation point, he may begin to continue his inquiry quite apart from a sense of identity with it. He is thus in danger of aligning with it to the point of losing sight of the questions that relate to his development as a human being. This may result in a loss of awareness of himself as the question.

When an individual loses awareness of himself in his involvement with an area, he does not penetrate into relevant meanings which are outside of the area. Actually, in this condition, he approaches a situation in which he loses concern about relevant meanings. When a person finds himself drifting into a type of numbness relative to a discipline, he should be helped to reflect intensively about this condition. It is hoped that the individual may always encounter conditions which will produce a true confrontation with this dilemma.

When one approaches a state of numbness with particular content, he needs to find new location places for meanings. When an individual reaches a saturation point in connection with a discipline, it simply means that the content has little or no relevance to himself as the question. For example, after having confronted the content in history to the point where it does not respond to him as the question, he will have to inquire into other areas. Not all messages will be generated in connection with one discipline. This is true especially if the discipline has been arranged along a lineal pattern by external authority. The individual has to break out of the discipline and seek other connections or relationships of meanings. As an individual, for example, finds himself encircled by historical movements and events, he will push out to the edge of the circle and attempt to ascertain the nature of the influences acting on himself and others involved. He will therefore discern the points which he may penetrate for the derivation of relevant meanings. In this endeavor he would liberate himself from the arrangement and enter into any and every content area which would have pertinence to his extended search for meanings. This may mean that he does or does not become attached to another discipline. There is no rule that suggests he must become involved with another discipline. It does suggest, however, that he may search into any content for meaningful conditions for the extension of his existence.

It is important to emphasize at this point that an individual could very well find relevance in the disciplines of knowledge and at the same time be liberated from any one or all of them as he inquires in depth into meanings to produce himself as well as others. This idea may appear paradoxical. Actually, the paradoxical condition here is most useful. If many of the elements of the science of biology have meaning to an individual's development, he will in turn bring greater vitality to this discipline of science without becoming encapsulated in it. Also, if one finds relevant meanings through items or conditions which cannot be associated with any discipline, he may be instrumental in either building a new discipline or expanding an established discipline. The individual here will renew his vitality as a human being and in turn bring new vitality to the content of the discipline.

An individual liberates himself toward more and extended contact points for meanings when he separates himself from himself and the external world and at the same time retains a sense of continuity with the world. In this liberation he comes into contact with many phenomena associated with people, nature, classrooms, schools, objects, art forms, animals, air, water, movement and others. He finds that his contacts with people may have relevance to his extended sense of existence. At times too he may find that these contacts may push toward a sense of dehumanization. He needs to relate himself to both conditions without losing his stance of separation. In order to produce himself and others, he will find as many meanings in one condition as the other. For example, as he ponders the question of people and their behavior, he may view the nature of their make-up—the sources of their vitality. He would probably consider how he exists as a unity. He would certainly not ignore his physical make-up—his bone structure which cradles and combines the many cells and the various organs at the center of his vitality. The contemplation of these structures leads one into a condition of inquiry about man as he exists as a physical being.

As one inquires about man as a physical being, he will become more conscious of himself as a physical being and extract messages from this inquiry toward a better knowledge of himself. Not the least of this inquiry would relate to questions relative to himself not only as a coordinated being but as one who extends his existence in ever so many ways. This inquiry could extend into the nature of the nervous system and its response to surrounding phenomena. Other forms of inquiry could relate to the mind and its interaction with the nervous system, bones, muscles and so on. Inquiry here must assume a direction more vital than an occupation with a physiological condition. It must relate to the contact with surrounding forces and movements. Many questions, for example, could develop in connection with inquiry about the nervous system as the antennae which will reveal the messages of the surrounding forces. Perhaps the nervous system is the radar system for the body. Through this system we may get at the basis of *what is.* Perhaps the impact may become so sharp that we would wish, as McLuhan suggests, to jump outside of ourselves. The mechanization of society may become too much to bear. This could be a warning system about serious interferences with the efforts to become more human.

As one considers the body, he may become increasingly conversant about its needs over and above nutrition. It may be revealing to become conscious of the many sources of food for the body. Much of this food may be found in conditions quite far removed from solids. Perhaps some of the greatest needs of bodies are satisfied through a continuity of contact between minds. The production of human beings goes beyond procreation. People need people in so many ways. The contact of the physical body, extended through mind, must occur with surrounding phenomena such as conversation, dialogue, shapes, forms, and other ways in order to attain the vitality which may be needed for greater existence and humanism. The effects of this contact extends to cells, organs, blood vessels, muscles, and all other elements of the body in unity with a sense of human realization. This is probably what is meant in part when one talks about becoming a healthy individual. To grow into greater health means encounters with more meanings rather than less. The more healthy individuals have not only more experiences with other individuals but also more intensive and extended ones. Their sense of curiosity grows day by day as they encounter more location places for inquiry with media, people, and the many aspects of their environment.

As one approaches himself as the question he searches for relevant meanings in many areas of knowledge. It should be clear from the foregoing discussion that ever so many experiences can emerge in connection with topics associated with one's everyday activities. This is not to say that one would wait for something to happen. Rather, when an individual has committed himself to a determined quest for relevant meanings, he may find at least initial realization in immediate situations. He then may intensify his inquiry so that through immediate situations he may encounter relevances in one or more disciplines. The individual could extend a discipline by virtue of intensified entrance to ideas separated from the discipline. On the other hand, the occupation with a discipline may strengthen the individual's inquiry through situations separated from it. His absorption with the discipline does not numb him as to what exists around him.

The conditions of learning should encourage students to approach disciplines with a vitality that would tend to extract new and extended meanings toward their sense of existence. The content in a study such as physics could be approached so as to reveal associations with the electronic age. Content that relates to locomotion would certainly be central to an understanding of the nature of the electronic age and its effects on human endeavor. One's relation to the subject-matter content of physics may tend to give him a sense of control of his existence. Then too he may begin to detect how this control may operate on him in a depreciative manner. When should locomotion be resisted and when encouraged? Are the perfection of motors an extension of man as a mobile creature? How is locomotion related to gravity and space orientation? How are motors related to the heart and mind of an individual? How do they affect the nervous system? How do they affect one's way of thinking about phenomena? The approach to these and other questions should certainly tend to promote vital experiences which are relevant to one's state of being.

When one puts himself into question, he will need to confront himself and the phenomena for a decision. This has been discussed to a considerable degree in other sections especially as an individual involves himself with various experiences. The question here is: How does one relate himself in the quest for a decision? In response to this question one is reminded of a most profound experience related by Buber about a young man who came to him for help. The young man came in the afternoon after Buber had experienced a morning of religious enthusiasm. Buber[2] speaks of the encounter with the young man in these words: "I conversed attentively and openly with him—only I omitted to guess the questions he did not put. I learned that he had come not for a chat but for a decision. What do we expect when we are in despair and yet go to a man? The young man did not ask other than by his presence, and he could not be answered other than by a presence given to him." The young man left with the questions he did not put. Later, Buber was told that the young man had died. The impact of this experience had a profound effect on Buber. It was, in fact, a turning point in his life. It was a conversion in reverse, so to speak, from religion to the condition of dialogue with the world. The dialogue, says Buber, need not be marked by words or speech, for the address of being, of being present in the moment of meeting, would suffice to disclose meaning and breach the wall of despair.

Buber cuts beneath the separateness of the world—the discrimination of subject-knowers and objects-known. He concerns himself with the human consequences of knowledge. What does knowledge do to man? How does man's way of knowing the world (science, art, etc.) affect his fundamental attitude towards the world? To the one in question the manner in which he comports himself before the world—how he stands, fixes himself, and presents himself to the world is of the greatest import. What is of moment is not how man, reflecting upon himself, determines his view of the world, but how man in the wholeness of his being places himself before the world. One needs to locate himself prior to the moment when each puts on his private mask and departs his separate way.

It needs to be continually emphasized that man in his separation of himself from himself and the universe puts himself in a position of relating to the world in that wholeness of being which involves him with the many secrets of the world. He thus begins to know the nature of the externality of the universe which tends to separate him from the world —which keeps him out of the moment of presence.

When an individual is not in separation with himself he is enveloped in the externals which numb him to the point of obscuring the world's secrets. He is separated from the world with all its meanings and can therefore not become involved with that content.

The schools tend to separate the individual from the world. The individual's route is determined. He is ordered into the regularities of the system. The condition prevents his involvement with the world. Since he is separated from this involvement, he is not in relation with

[2]Martin Buber, *Between Man and Man,* trans. by Ronald Gregor Smith, introduction by Maurice Friedman (New York: Macmillan, 1965), pp. 13-14.

knowledge in such a way as to respond to his existence. He is not in question.

We have talked a great deal about man separating himself from himself and from the universe in order to have the moment of presence before the world in an unmasked state. It is important that the individual in this separation and being in question produces this same condition with the school. Actually, he cannot fail to bring the school into question. In his examination of his state of encapsulation with the school and its regularities, he will transform the picture he has held about the school. As he presents himself unmasked before the world, he will thereby bring the school to be open and receptive to the messages of the world.

As suggested before, in order to keep alive and extend the sense of liberation in which lies the quality of mind, it would appear necessary to go beyond and outside of the disciplines to build content for the approach to relevant meanings. As individuals become involved with these endeavors, there would come into being all types of location places for the pursuit of meanings. The location places have not been predesigned and will therefore be encountered as individuals search for meaning. It is impossible to state ahead of the encounter what the centers or location places for meaning will be and what effect they may have on individuals.

As individuals put themselves into question, they open themselves to the forces which are clamoring for entrance into the conditions for inquiry. Actually, the impinging forces will tend to become the conditions and must be part of the concern of every individual. Individuals, as they are involved with the conditions, become the human antennae for the messages which are multiple and real. It would be presumptuous on the part of one to label the messages which may be received by another. One point, however, would be quite certain and that is that the labels of most messages would have little or no resemblance to the units of learning—courses and programs of instruction usually designed in schools and colleges. These appear to have a familiar ring such as English I, English II, English Composition, English Literature and so on. The subject matter is approached as if it is a settled arrangement. Does it really suggest a sense of awareness to the real when someone says "Next semester we will study English, American, or some other literature"? Actually the approach to literature suggested by this statement is that the content and the individual is separated. The individual would certainly not approach it as the question or as a first behaver in inquiring into it.

The predesignated approach to subject-matter content indicated above is conspicuous for its disregard of the individual and his sense of

identity with meaning. It is obvious that the individual who was responsible for this had not put himself into question in his manner of inquiry.
At the same time he did not conceive of anyone else being in question.
The key to the drift into dealing with irrelevancies is the study of a unit,
subject, or program without being concerned about what it does to one.

As one regards himself as the question as well as helping others to
view themselves as questions, he begins to look for messages and elements of impact which relate to an individual's definition of himself.
Some possible examples from which this impact may come are the
electronic world, the poets, and artists, the world in ferment, the state
of humanism, the nature of arrangements for control, perspectives in
communication, the new revolution, the elements of alienation, the
programming of minds, the new relevances, and others. The ideas coming from any one of these categories would be related to many of those
of the other categories.

The categories suggested as possible examples that might generate impact would pose many social hangups and many predicaments of
all kinds. For example, the development of relationships with the electronic world would bring into question the how and why of survival.
More important, what are the elements of depreciation as well as elevation of human existence which are resident in the electronic environment? In the ever-increasing contact points for existence in this
environment, how does an individual find relevances for himself in
furthering his sense of self-actualization? How may an individual confront with the electronic world so as to expand his contact points for the
search of meaning? Is he becoming sufficiently aware of its effects so
that he is not encapsulated by it? Is the electronic world making him
a child of that world or is it providing the instrumentation whereby he
may attain a renewed sense of vitality? What were the influences, his-
toric and otherwise, which brought the individual into the electronic
condition? Individuals in the secondary schools and colleges and uni-
versities need to relate to questions of the type indicated. It is the
responsibility of individuals to help develop the conditions where each
one becomes a first behaver in inquiring into the sources which may
produce wisdom regarding the type of questions which are indicated.

Poets, artists, and others have always tried to depict the human
condition so that a sobering wisdom may result to men. Some have been
attuned to the messages and have become first behavers as artists and
poets. Others have become engulfed into the sweep of systems and
arrangements and are thus unaware as to the consequences to them.
They simply respond to the "this is the way it is" type of thinking. These
are the ones who approach knowledge as courses in History—American,
English, Medieval—as courses in English I, English II, and American or

English Literature and so on. The same is true with the sciences and mathematics. They either hope for illumination from the courses and other programmed arrangements or have separated themselves as individuals from the courses and disciplines. They just have not put themselves into question and thus remain unaware as to possible effects of courses and planned systems in their further involvement with them. They have become so engulfed with the tenacious arrangement that they neither seek nor find time to recapture thought relative to them.

There are others who are asking many questions about man's state, whether it be that of liberation or that of incarceration. They will look into the nature of dialogue, for example, as a possible new perspective in communication. They will begin to view the importance of relating to people as minds, both to give and receive. They will relate to all media including books, objects, film and phenomena—natural and otherwise. They will confront with others not only to receive meaning relative to differences in people but to expand and elevate those differences. There will be a continuous effort at expanding the areas for inquiry. As individuals approach meanings for their individual revitalization, they will at the same time expand and redevelop the existing disciplines of knowledge and bring about new ones.

The world has much to reveal and give to individuals if they will stand in its presence. This means that they will have to separate themselves from the arrangements and view themselves—where they have been, what it was like, and where they might go. As they put themselves into dialogue with the world, they may relate to questions such as the following: Why do we produce and follow irrelevancies and yet experience no real concern about this behavior? Why do we choose to be comfortable at the expense of the vitality of original forms when all the world was unmasked before us? How can we recapture the moments of greatness which now have become dreams? In relating to the search for meaning associated with these questions, individuals may have to view men and phenomena in their unmasked state and begin again to produce themselves. For example, in considering all the sources and relationships which influence him into his present ways of living, an individual can extract some of the elements to further his own sense of existence, and alter others so as to introduce new possibilities of living. Attempts would be made to probe the "moments" in the lives of individuals which produced a greater sense of liberation to inquire about a better existence. How was love a factor in producing that dialogue which revealed a direction to a greater sense of humaness among individuals? At the same time what were the factors which produced violence as an avenue of man's relation to man?

An authentic approach to these questions and predicaments has to be in terms of man as the question. He needs to relate himself to other minds so that meaning comes to him as well as to others. He soon discovers that he has to relate to minds of the past. He communes in thought with the poet so as to extend himself across times and places. He needs to place himself unmasked before the knowledge which has already been conceived and try to ascertain its continuity with his own being. He then goes in and out of knowledge as disciplines so as to weave it around himself as the question. This would then transform both the knowledge and himself in a sense of mutual integrity.

What has been described and discussed in the foregoing pages is sum and substance of all the disciplines of knowledge. The manner of the thinking here should be obvious—that the individual and the disciplines become mutually related. Each deals with each other and the disciplines in such a manner that there is no separation from the individual as the question. Yet there is an absence of institutional codification of the ideas which are internalized by the individual. The ideas help produce the individual even as he produces the ideas.

SELECTED READINGS

Cummings, E. E. *Six Non-Lectures.* New York: Atheneum, 1963, pp. 42-98.

Friedenberg, Edgar Z. *Coming of Age in America.* New York: Random House, 1965.

Jackson, P. W. "The Student's World." Mimeo. University of Chicago, 1966.

King, Arthur R., Jr., and John A. Brownell. *The Curriculum and the Disciplines of Knowledge.* New York: Wiley, 1966.

Lear, John. "A New Look at the Human Mind," *Saturday Review,* April 1, 1961.

Leeper, Robert R. (ed.). *Humanizing Education: The Person in the Process.* Washington, D. C.: Association for Super-and Curriculum Development, NEA, 1967.

———. (ed.). *Educational Leadership,* Vol. 26, No. 8 (May 1969). pp. 749-760.

Muessing, Raymond H. (ed.). *Youth Education—Problems/Perspectives/Promises.* Washington, D.C.: Association for Supervision and Curriculum Development, 1968, pp. 46-84.

Rubin, Lois J. (ed.). *Life Skills in School and Society.* Washington, D.C.: Association for Supervision and Cirriculum Development, NEA, 1969.

Index